I hope you enjoy my designs!

MEET THE BUILDER

Jessica Farrell designed and created all of the houses in this book. She is a professional brick artist from Ireland whose models are displayed at events around the world.

When did you first start building? At the age of four, when my mother gave me my first LEGO® set. I am very grateful because she started a lifelong love and future career.

What's your favourite LEGO® piece? The jumper plate. It enables you to add lots of detail to builds by "offsetting" pieces by half a stud. I once built a model that used almost 7,000 jumper plates!

Which house in this book would you most like to live in? The fairy house, shaped like a mushroom (page 24). It's small but it's magical, so I imagine it has hundreds of rooms inside!

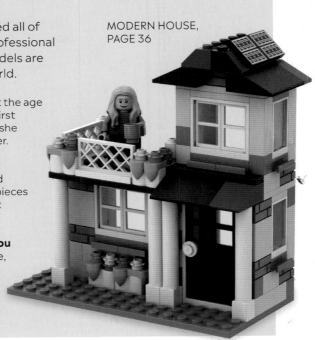
MODERN HOUSE, PAGE 36

Rounded toe of the boot

OLD BOOT HOUSE, PAGE 74

HOW TO BEGIN

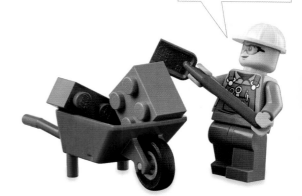

Got my bricks. What's next?

This book is all about building LEGO® houses, from their foundations to the tips of their roofs. Some are high up in the trees, while others are perched on the seashore. There are colourful gingerbread and rainbow houses, and even a flying home. The houses start off easy and become harder as you move through the book, making it one imaginative building journey. Are you ready to begin?

BREAKING DOWN BUILDING

Each house is broken down into three to five important building stages. You might not have all the bricks you need, but you don't have to copy the models brick by brick. The breakdowns show techniques to inspire your own amazing ideas. There are also "ideas galleries" that focus on particular parts of houses, such as doors and roofs, and ways to expand your builds.

The first picture is always the finished model

Each model is classed as easy, medium, or hard

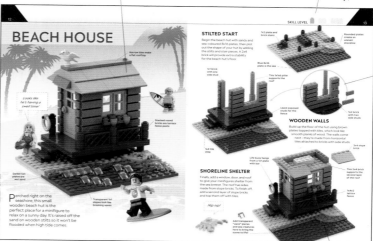

Some parts of models are broken down even more in these circles

HOUSE MODEL

The last step is one of the final stages – usually the roof

Smaller parts of house models or extra build ideas

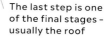

IDEAS GALLERY

BRICK LISTS

If you'd like to see all of the bricks used in a particular house model, go to
www.dk.com/legohouses

How To Build
LEGO®
Houses

**Written by
Hannah Dolan**

**Models by
Jessica Farrell**

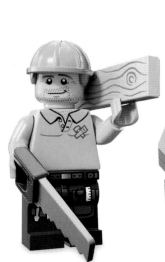
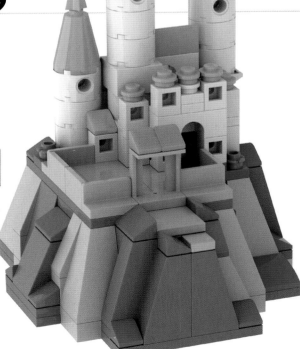

CONTENTS

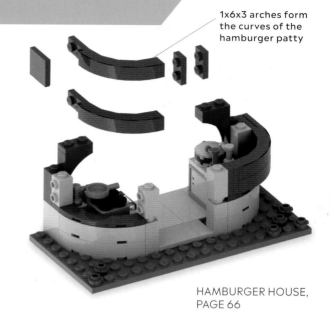

1x6x3 arches form the curves of the hamburger patty

HAMBURGER HOUSE, PAGE 66

FLYING HOUSE, PAGE 72

Flight controls

TECHNICAL TIPS

These notes for builders will help you to understand some
of the LEGO words and terms that are used a lot in this book.

LEGO® DICTIONARY

Studs are the round, raised bumps on top of bricks and plates. They fit into "tubes" on the bottom of pieces.

2x3 brick

Bricks are found in most LEGO models, especially houses! They are named according to how many studs they have on top.

1x2 brick

Plates are similar to bricks because they have studs on top and tubes on the bottom, but they are much thinner.

1x3 plate

Tiles are thin, like plates, but they have no studs on top.

2x2 tile

Holes inside bricks and other pieces can hold connectors like pins, bars, and axles.

1x2 brick with LEGO® Technic hole

WAYS TO BUILD

1x4 plate attached underneath

Downwards
You can add pieces underneath parts of your houses to make them more secure.

Upwards
The "easy" houses in this book mostly show pieces stacked on top of each other like this.

1x2 brick with two side studs

Hinge plates attach to hinge bricks to form the roof shape

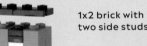

Sideways
For more advanced models, you can use pieces with studs on their sides to build sideways.

All angles
Build moving parts or interesting shapes into your houses using hinged pieces or clips and bars.

HOW BIG IS YOUR HOUSE?

Modular builds
You could build multiple homes, like a block of flats or a row of houses, using modular building techniques.

Minifigure scale
If you want minifigures to live inside your house, think about how wide or tall your minifigure residents are and how they would move around within it.

Microscale
This is anything smaller than minifigure scale, often using fewer pieces. You can imagine your tiny homeowners inside!

SIMPLE HOUSE

This little dwelling is for minifigures and builders who enjoy the simple things in life. Its perfectly square proportions make this a good one to start with if you're new to house-building. The house and garden are all built on one 16x16 base plate.

If you live simply, you have more time for fun hobbies.

Like kendo. Let's go, Dad!

1x1 round brick chimney pot

The roof has three layers of slope bricks

Simple cool yellow brick walls

2x2x4 prickly bush

Tile and jumper plate garden path

The green base plate is the lawn

SQUARE ON SQUARE

The square simple house fits neatly into the corner of its square base plate. The bottom layer of the walls is made from grey masonry bricks, and cool yellow bricks form the second layer. At this point, plot out the garden details too, like mounds of grass and the paved path.

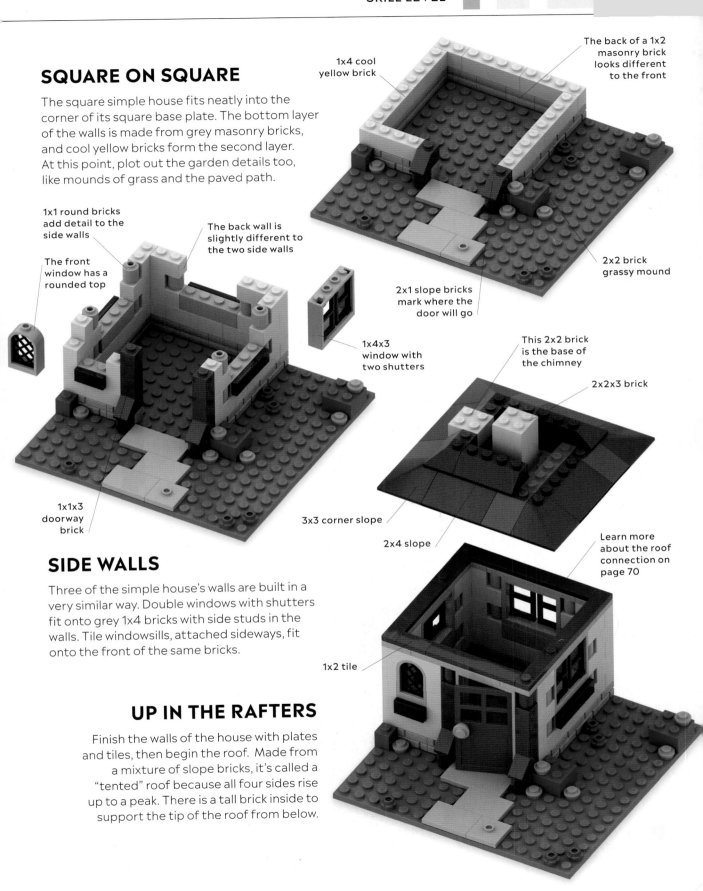

1x4 cool yellow brick

The back of a 1x2 masonry brick looks different to the front

1x1 round bricks add detail to the side walls

The back wall is slightly different to the two side walls

The front window has a rounded top

2x2 brick grassy mound

2x1 slope bricks mark where the door will go

1x4x3 window with two shutters

This 2x2 brick is the base of the chimney

2x2x3 brick

1x1x3 doorway brick

3x3 corner slope

2x4 slope

Learn more about the roof connection on page 70

SIDE WALLS

Three of the simple house's walls are built in a very similar way. Double windows with shutters fit onto grey 1x4 bricks with side studs in the walls. Tile windowsills, attached sideways, fit onto the front of the same bricks.

1x2 tile

UP IN THE RAFTERS

Finish the walls of the house with plates and tiles, then begin the roof. Made from a mixture of slope bricks, it's called a "tented" roof because all four sides rise up to a peak. There is a tall brick inside to support the tip of the roof from below.

LOG CABIN

Deep in the LEGO® woods lies this traditional log cabin. It has walls made from horizontal logs that interlock at the corners. Minifigures come here to get away from it all and relax by the tranquil waters of the lake... but the local wildlife seems to have other ideas!

Tiles at alternating heights create a corrugated metal roof

If you don't have tree pieces, you could build your own trees

Wooden supporting post made from 1x1 round bricks

That wasn't in the brochure!

Grey pieces look like rocks

A double curved slope and two eyes are the submerged body of a lake monster!

Open fire is a flame piece on a 1x1 round plate

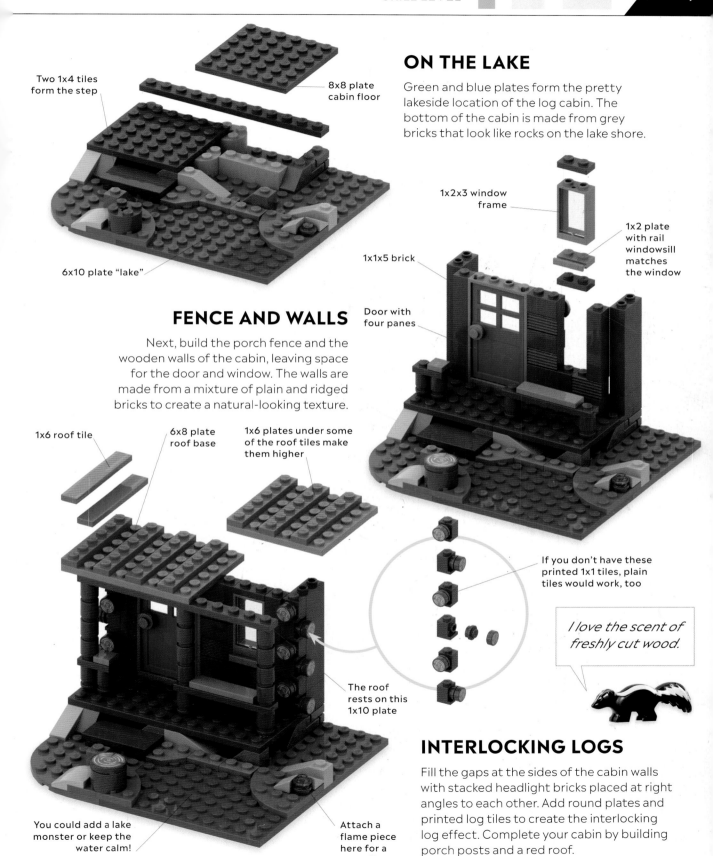

Two 1x4 tiles form the step

8x8 plate cabin floor

ON THE LAKE

Green and blue plates form the pretty lakeside location of the log cabin. The bottom of the cabin is made from grey bricks that look like rocks on the lake shore.

6x10 plate "lake"

1x2x3 window frame

1x2 plate with rail windowsill matches the window

1x1x5 brick

FENCE AND WALLS

Next, build the porch fence and the wooden walls of the cabin, leaving space for the door and window. The walls are made from a mixture of plain and ridged bricks to create a natural-looking texture.

Door with four panes

1x6 roof tile

6x8 plate roof base

1x6 plates under some of the roof tiles make them higher

If you don't have these printed 1x1 tiles, plain tiles would work, too

I love the scent of freshly cut wood.

The roof rests on this 1x10 plate

INTERLOCKING LOGS

Fill the gaps at the sides of the cabin walls with stacked headlight bricks placed at right angles to each other. Add round plates and printed log tiles to create the interlocking log effect. Complete your cabin by building porch posts and a red roof.

You could add a lake monster or keep the water calm!

Attach a flame piece here for a camp fire

COLOURS AND TEXTURES

Plain LEGO walls look great and serve their purpose perfectly, but building in more texture and colour can take your house-building to the next level. Try out some of these wall techniques to give your homes a more natural or unusual look.

SIMPLE CHANGES

Adding just one other colour to a plain wall can make a big difference to the look of it. This country cottage has lots of "palisade" bricks in a colour (nougat) that works well with yellow. The curved edges of the palisade bricks create texture, too.

The roof slopes are two shades of red

1x2 palisade brick

Place the different colours at irregular intervals

GARDEN WALLS

This is a garden wall for the indecisive homeowner! It shows four different ways to create interesting textures, including a shell wall and a ridged red-brick design.

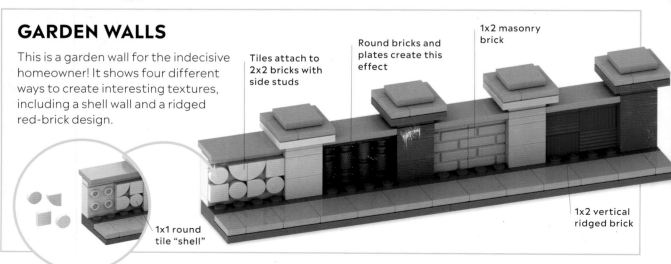

Tiles attach to 2x2 bricks with side studs

Round bricks and plates create this effect

1x2 masonry brick

1x1 round tile "shell"

1x2 vertical ridged brick

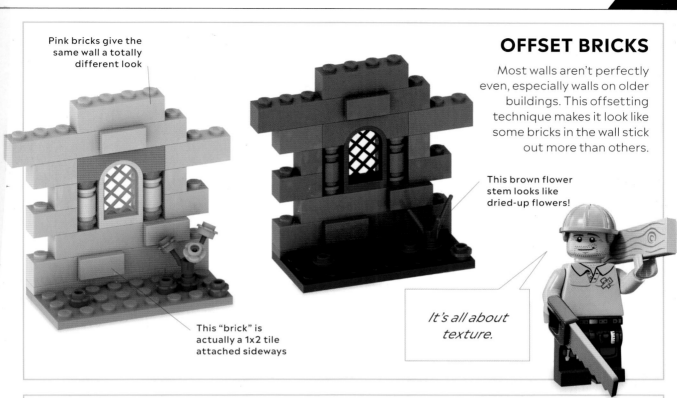

Pink bricks give the same wall a totally different look

OFFSET BRICKS

Most walls aren't perfectly even, especially walls on older buildings. This offsetting technique makes it look like some bricks in the wall stick out more than others.

This brown flower stem looks like dried-up flowers!

This "brick" is actually a 1x2 tile attached sideways

It's all about texture.

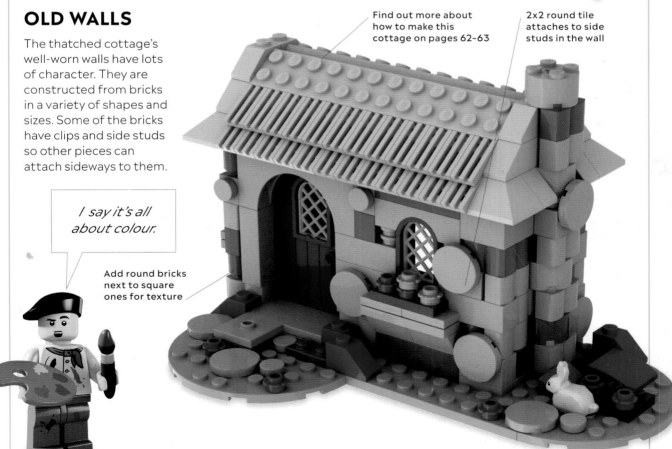

OLD WALLS

The thatched cottage's well-worn walls have lots of character. They are constructed from bricks in a variety of shapes and sizes. Some of the bricks have clips and side studs so other pieces can attach sideways to them.

I say it's all about colour.

Add round bricks next to square ones for texture

Find out more about how to make this cottage on pages 62–63

2x2 round tile attaches to side studs in the wall

BEACH HOUSE

Narrow tiles make
a flat rooftop

Looks like
he's having a
swell time!

Stacked round
bricks are terrace
fence posts

Darker tan
plates are
wet sand

Transparent 1x1
slopes look like
breaking waves

Perched right on the seashore, this small wooden beach hut is the perfect place for a minifigure to relax on a sunny day. It's raised off the sand on wooden stilts so it won't be flooded when high tide comes.

STILTED START

Begin the beach hut with sandy and sea-coloured 8x16 plates, then plot out the shape of your hut by adding the stilts and stair pieces. A 2x4 brick will provide extra stability for the beach hut's floor.

1x2 plate and brick stairs

Rounded plates create an uneven shoreline

Blue 8x16 plate is the sea

1x1 brick with one side stud

This 1x1x6 pillar supports the roof

Leave exposed studs for the fence

1x2 brick with two side studs

1x4 tile step

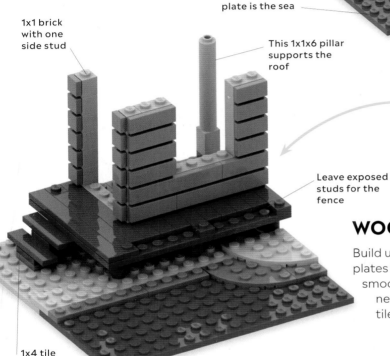

WOODEN WALLS

Build up the floor of the hut using brown plates topped with tiles, which look like smooth planks of wood. The walls come next – they're made from horizontal tiles attached to bricks with side studs.

3x4 slope brick

Life buoy hangs from a 1x1 plate with bar

This 2x4 brick supports the second layer of the roof

SHORELINE SHELTER

Finally, add a window, door, and roof to give your minifigures shelter from the sea breeze. The roof has sides made from slope bricks. To finish off, add a second layer of slope bricks and top them off with tiles.

1x4x2 lattice fence

Nip nip!

Add transparent "wave" pieces and sea creatures here to bring the scene to life!

COUNTRY COTTAGE

Chimney stack
splits open

Bright and dark red
slope bricks form
the tiled roof

1x4 hinge brick

1x4 plate
window box

*I'll huff and I'll
puff and
I'll split your
house open!*

This simple country home is easy to build and even easier to play inside, thanks to hinge pieces in the chimney stack. They allow the front and back walls of the house to open up. The back part of the house has a matching blue window and another window box filled with flowers.

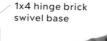

TWO SIDES

The country cottage is built on two identical 6x12 plates. Plan out the shape of the home by attaching the lowest bricks of the walls to each plate. Also make a start on the splitting chimney stack.

1x4 hinge brick swivel top

1x4 hinge brick swivel base

2x2 round tile doorstep

1x1 plate sits under half of the hinge brick

Small slopes are long grass in the garden

1x4x3 window with shutters

1x4 brick

Stacked 1x1 bricks

2x4 plate windowsill

MATCHING WINDOWS

The yellow and nougat brick walls of the cottage are taking shape and it's time for the identical windows to be fitted into them. Build up the chimney stack at the same time as the walls.

Inverted 2x1 bricks support the windowsills

Each step of the side wall is one stud wide

STEPPED ROOF

Once the windows and front door are in place, begin the roof section. This simple roof is mostly made from 2x4 slope bricks. They are supported by small, stepped bricks on either side of both parts of the cottage.

2x4 slope brick

1x2 brick

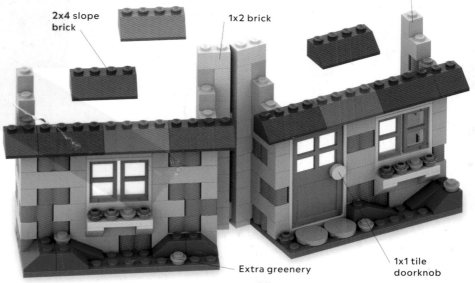

Extra greenery

1x1 tile doorknob

DOORS

A door is a very important part of any LEGO home – and not just because it's the way in! It can also add a lot of personality. Will you choose single or double doors, a modern glass or wooden door, or something altogether different?

White-framed window matches the door

It's just a-door-able!

STREET DOORWAYS

A row of doorways may be all you need to make a street scene. Adding different 1x1 round tiles and plates to make doorknobs can give doors a distinctive look.

SIMPLE DOOR

There are lots of ready-made LEGO door pieces to choose from. A plain white door fits in well with this simply designed red-brick cottage.

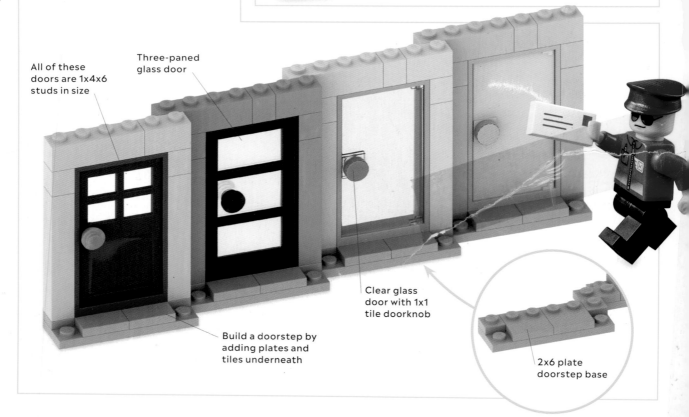

All of these doors are 1x4x6 studs in size

Three-paned glass door

Clear glass door with 1x1 tile doorknob

Build a doorstep by adding plates and tiles underneath

2x6 plate doorstep base

JAIL DOOR

The barred door on this cave identifies it as a jungle jail cell! Or perhaps it's a place to hide from dangerous dinosaurs. The door fits inside a grey doorframe, which blends in with the grey and beige rocks around it.

Jungle vine attached to a green headlight brick

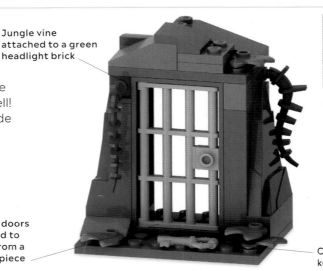

I had to wait until the Iron Age to put this door on my cave.

Many LEGO doors are designed to swing out from a doorframe piece

Could this key open the cell door?

It's only me! I forgot my key.

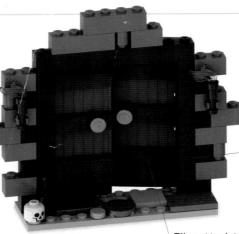

FORTRESS DOOR

The towering wooden doors of a fortress are designed to deter any unwelcome visitors. These double doors have hinges on opposite sides. They attach to bricks with clips built into the walls.

Black doorframe made from bricks

1x1x3 brick with two clips

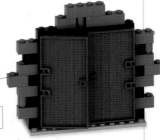

BACK VIEW

Tiles attach to rows of studs on the door

SWING DOORS

Any Wild West saloon needs swing doors for heroes and villains to burst into or out of! These door pieces can swivel both outwards and inwards when they're attached to bricks with clips.

Traditional arched doorway could also be square

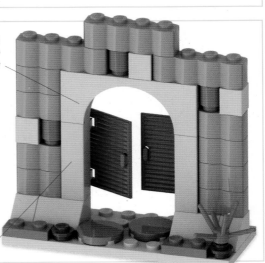

1x1x3 brick has two clips at the back

BUNGALOW

This charming microscale bungalow is built using small bricks, tiles, and plates in inventive ways. It's small in size but big on details, with a wooden front door, a perfectly paved driveway, and a colourful garden with manicured hedges.

2x2 double slope bricks and other sloped pieces form the top layer of the gable roof

Garden blooms made from 1x1 round plates with petals

1x1 round tiles form the winding garden path

Tan bricks and plates create a natural stone effect

Hedges are 1x2 tiles with vertical teeth

The driveway is made from four 1x2 grille tiles

This house is the perfect size for my rubber duck!

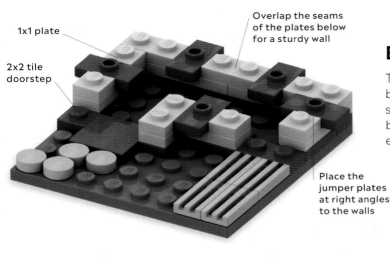

1x1 plate

2x2 tile
doorstep

Overlap the seams
of the plates below
for a sturdy wall

Place the
jumper plates
at right angles
to the walls

BUNGALOW BRICKWORK

The whole bungalow is built on one 8x8 base plate, with foundations made from smaller plates and tiles. The second layer of brickwork includes jumper plates – their edges form the bungalow's tiny windowsills.

INSIDE, OUTSIDE, ON ITS SIDE

Both of the bungalow's doors are built using sideways-building techniques, while its neat, square windows are headlight bricks facing inwards.

1x1x2 brick
with two
side studs

1x2 tile

1x2 ridged
brick

2x2 corner
brick

Headlight
brick

1x2x2 brick
with four
side studs

2x2 corner
slope brick

1x2 slope
brick

A 4x8 plate
ceiling holds up
the roof

2x2 slope
brick

GABLE ROOF

The bungalow has a gable roof, which means it has two sloped roof sections built in opposite directions. It's made from two layers of sloped bricks in various shapes and sizes.

2x2 tile
garage door

Think of something big in a garden and work out how to build it small.

LIGHTHOUSE

Ships look out for this lighthouse's bright, flashing beacon of light at night. It tells them where land is so they can steer clear of hazardous rocks. The lighthouse's red-and-white striped tower has a lantern room for its powerful lamp at the top and an adjoining lighthouse keeper's cottage at the bottom.

Lantern room balcony

Red and white stripes are easy for ships to spot

Hey, I've just washed that roof! Pesky gulls.

Grey slopes are craggy rocks

Small transparent pieces look like swirling water

ROCKY BASE

The lighthouse is built on a base that's half-land, half-sea thanks to large dark grey and blue plates. The sharp, uneven-looking rocks on the coastline are made from slope pieces in different sizes, placed at right angles.

1x4 bricks build up the base for the lighthouse

3x1 slope brick

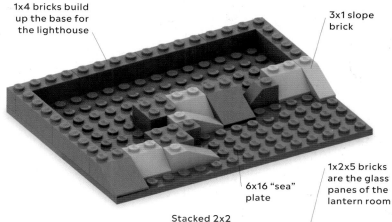

6x16 "sea" plate

1x2x5 bricks are the glass panes of the lantern room

Stacked 2x2 round bricks are the lantern

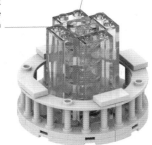

LAND AHOY!

After adding a layer of grey plates onto the rocky base, add grass and a paved path on the land. Then begin building the bottom of the lighthouse and the walls of the keeper's cottage.

Each layer of the lighthouse is built in a similar way

Read more about the lighthouse tower on page 41

This layer of plates supports the roof

Simple walls made from blue bricks

Black bricks at the bottom match the lighthouse

Overhanging curved bricks make the coastline look more natural

2x2 "macaroni" bricks form the curved edges of the tower

2x2 double concave slope

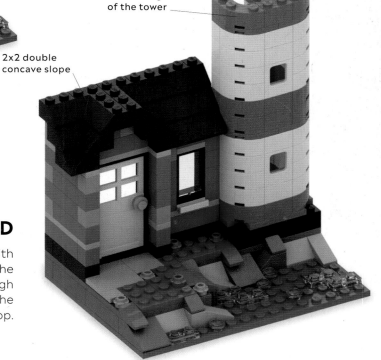

BEACON BUILD

Finish off the keeper's cottage with a black roof, then build up the lighthouse tower. Once it's tall enough to see for miles out to sea, build the light-filled lantern room at the top.

WINDOWS

A LEGO® house wouldn't be a home without windows. They let the light in and let minifigures look out on their surroundings. There's a whole world of LEGO window pieces and a multitude of ways to build them into walls.

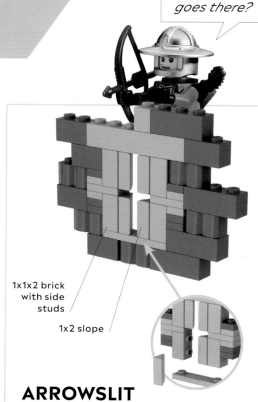

Halt! Who goes there?

CASTLE WINDOW

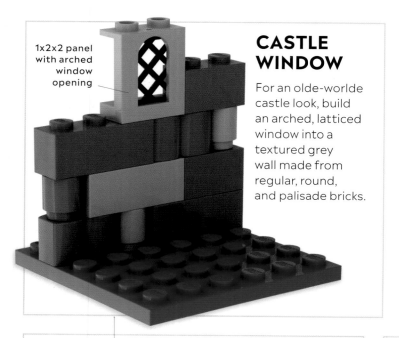

1x2x2 panel with arched window opening

For an olde-worlde castle look, build an arched, latticed window into a textured grey wall made from regular, round, and palisade bricks.

1x1x2 brick with side studs

1x2 slope

ARROWSLIT

Look out! Archers shoot arrows from these long, narrow windows, which are found on many castles. The cross-shaped gap is made using four slope bricks attached to bricks with side studs.

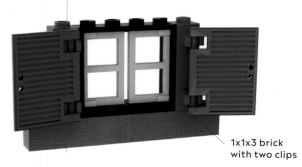

1x1x3 brick with two clips

SHUTTERED WINDOW

Some windows have shutters to protect them from bad weather, to control the sunlight, and because they look nice! To add them to your designs, build in bricks with side clips on either side of a window.

Jumper plates are two studs wide with one stud in the middle

RECESSED WINDOW

Sometimes windows sit slightly inside the walls that surround them. This recessed window style is built into a two-stud-wide wall but attached with jumper plates at the top and bottom.

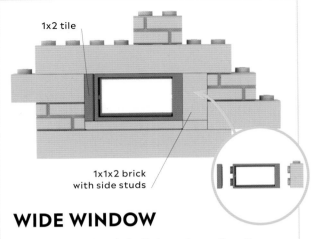

1x2 tile

1x1x2 brick
with side studs

WIDE WINDOW

This wide window is built into the wall on its side thanks to a brick with side studs. Adding a tile in the same colour on the left side of the window frame makes it look more symmetrical.

1x4 hinge brick

BAY WINDOW

Bay windows project out from a wall to create a light-filled living space. The three separate window panels on this build are joined together and to the wall with hinge bricks to give the window its protruding shape.

SHOP WINDOWS

A good shop window needs to tempt passing customers inside by displaying the shop's best wares. The large windows on this row of shops are all built by combining multiple window pieces.

Elongate arched windows by adding square ones below

Match the window styles of the first-floor flats with the shop windows below

FAIRY HOUSE

Never step on a toadstool when out walking in the woods – it may just be a fairy's home, like this one! The mushroom's recognizable red cap with white spots is its tiny roof, with a fairy-built chimney poking out. There's a large door built into the mushroom's stem for welcoming tiny visitors.

3x3 radar dish is the chimney lid

"Cheese" slopes and curved slopes form the top layer of the roof

Round-top door with latticed window

So this next house is one of our most unique properties.

It's nice but there's not mush-room.

Green base plates are the forest floor

1x1 plates with petals are tiny plants or moss

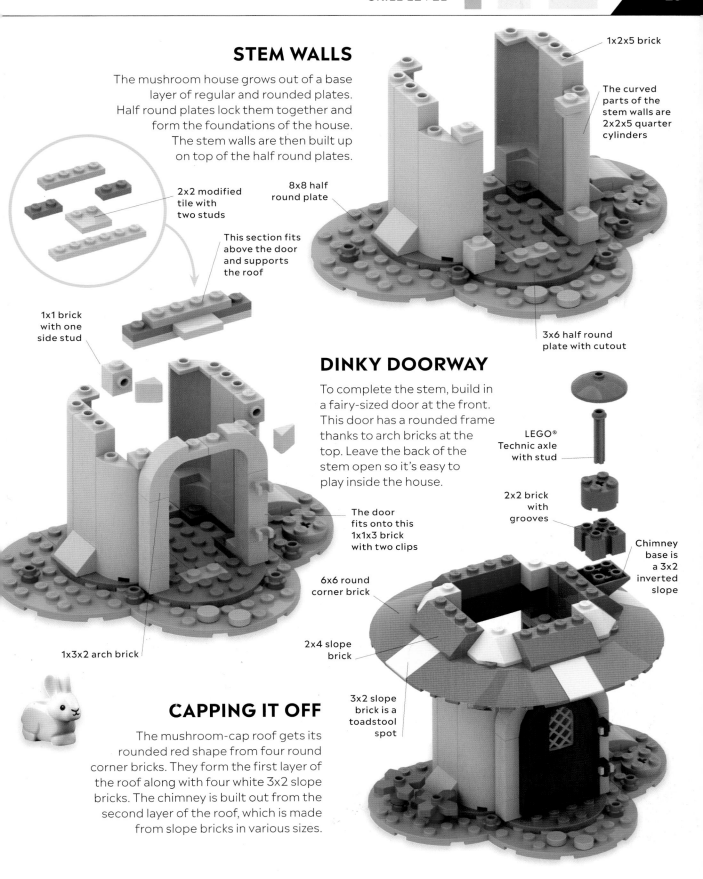

STEM WALLS

The mushroom house grows out of a base layer of regular and rounded plates. Half round plates lock them together and form the foundations of the house. The stem walls are then built up on top of the half round plates.

2x2 modified tile with two studs

8x8 half round plate

1x2x5 brick

The curved parts of the stem walls are 2x2x5 quarter cylinders

This section fits above the door and supports the roof

1x1 brick with one side stud

3x6 half round plate with cutout

DINKY DOORWAY

To complete the stem, build in a fairy-sized door at the front. This door has a rounded frame thanks to arch bricks at the top. Leave the back of the stem open so it's easy to play inside the house.

LEGO® Technic axle with stud

2x2 brick with grooves

The door fits onto this 1x1x3 brick with two clips

Chimney base is a 3x2 inverted slope

6x6 round corner brick

2x4 slope brick

3x2 slope brick is a toadstool spot

1x3x2 arch brick

CAPPING IT OFF

The mushroom-cap roof gets its rounded red shape from four round corner bricks. They form the first layer of the roof along with four white 3x2 slope bricks. The chimney is built out from the second layer of the roof, which is made from slope bricks in various sizes.

FESTIVE HOUSE

This cosy home is a welcome sight in the cold and dark days and nights of winter. Illuminated with colourful lights, a freshly built snowman, and frosted foliage, it's beautifully decorated inside and out for the festive season.

Colourful fairy lights are light bulb pieces

White pieces in the roof look like snow

Chimney stack promises a warming fire inside

1x1 round tiles create snow-covered plants

Garden Christmas tree

Have you seen the broom?

White tiles and plates are patches of snow

1x1 round plates are burning embers in the fireplace

INSIDE AND OUT

The base of the festive house is one big 16x16 plate. If you don't have one, you could use smaller plates as most of the base plate isn't visible. It's covered by tiles and snowy plates on the outside, and more tiles for the wooden floor and cosy rug on the inside.

Narrow tiles form the rug

1x2 ridged bricks make interesting walls

1x1 brackets have side studs to hang stockings from

WINTRY WALLS

Now build the two walls and add a door to keep out the cold winter air. The fireplace around the fire is the perfect place to hang Christmas stockings from, so include pieces with side studs to attach them to.

Add 1x1x6 columns either side of the doorframe

1x6x2 arch brick

You can see more of the interior on page 93

INSIDE VIEW

Headlight brick

1x2 brick with side studs

The slope bricks for the roof will attach here

Light bulb pieces fit onto the side studs

LIGHTS ON

Build up the chimney stack on the outside wall using regular and slope bricks in two shades of grey. Some of the bricks have side studs with tiles attached to create an uneven surface. Finish off the walls using more bricks with side studs to attach multicoloured fairy lights to.

The tree is built around two 1x1 bricks with studs on four sides

1x2 tile attached sideways

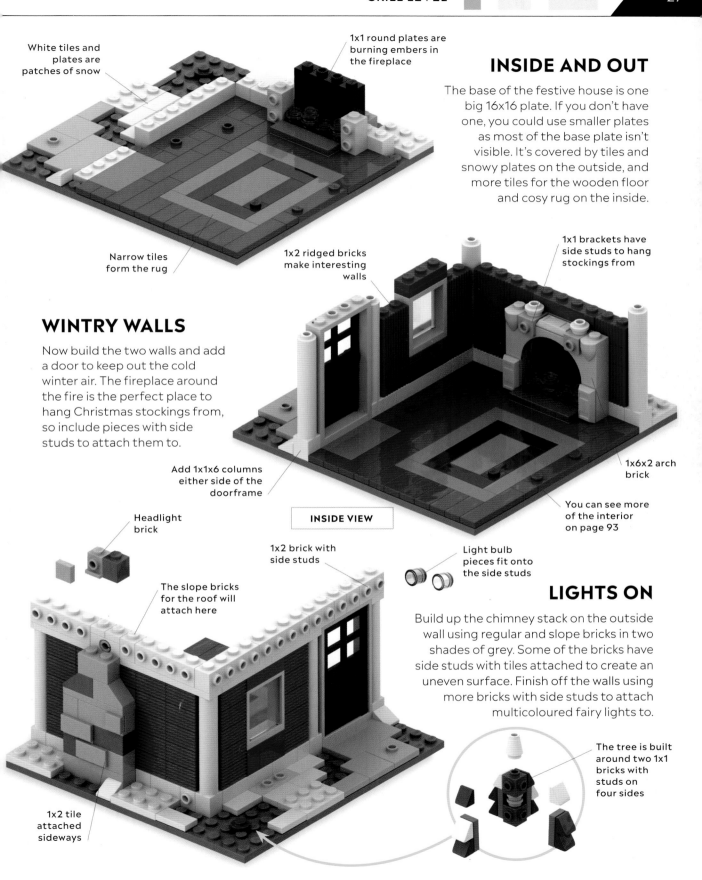

ROOFS

A strong and sturdy roof is a must on any minifigure home because it provides warmth and protection from the elements. Roofs might all do the same job, but that doesn't mean they have to look the same. Here are five very different roof techniques to inspire your LEGO house-building.

Brick-built side walls support the steps of the roof

1x1 plates make alternate rows higher

1x2 slope brick

BACK VIEW

Modified 4x4 tile with studs on the edge

2x2x3 corner slope

MEDITERRANEAN STYLE

Homes in the warm climate of the Mediterranean often have roofs made from tiles of terracotta, which is a type of clay. This Mediterranean-inspired roof is constructed from stepped layers of dark red 1x2 slope bricks.

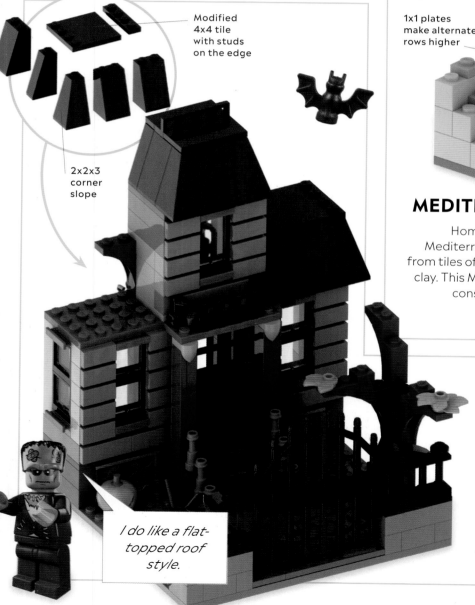

I do like a flat-topped roof style.

MANSARD ROOF

This haunted house has a mansard roof, which means each of its three black roof sections has a flat top and sloping sides. Their exposed edges are made from slope bricks in different sizes with tiles, modified tiles, and plates on top.

Periscope fits onto a 2x2 tile with pin

4x6 car bonnet wedge plate

RUSTIC ROOF

This yellow straw roof is made from 4x8 plates, which are held at an angle by a hinge connection underneath. Lots of yellow and bright light-orange slopes in different sizes create the thatched straw effect on top.

1x2 hinge brick and plate connection

The side of the roof is built from bricks

Bright light-orange 1x2 slope

UNUSUAL ROOF

The underwater house's roof is made almost entirely from car bonnet pieces! It's fun to think outside the box and use pieces in unusual ways, especially on imaginative builds like this one. You can see more of this house on pages 68–69.

2x4 hinge plate top

SLOPING ROOF

Like the rustic roof above, the winter chalet's large, steeply sloping roof plates are angled from underneath using hinge connections. The plates rest on the triangular-shaped front wall of the first floor of the chalet.

6x16 plate

2x4 hinge plate bottom

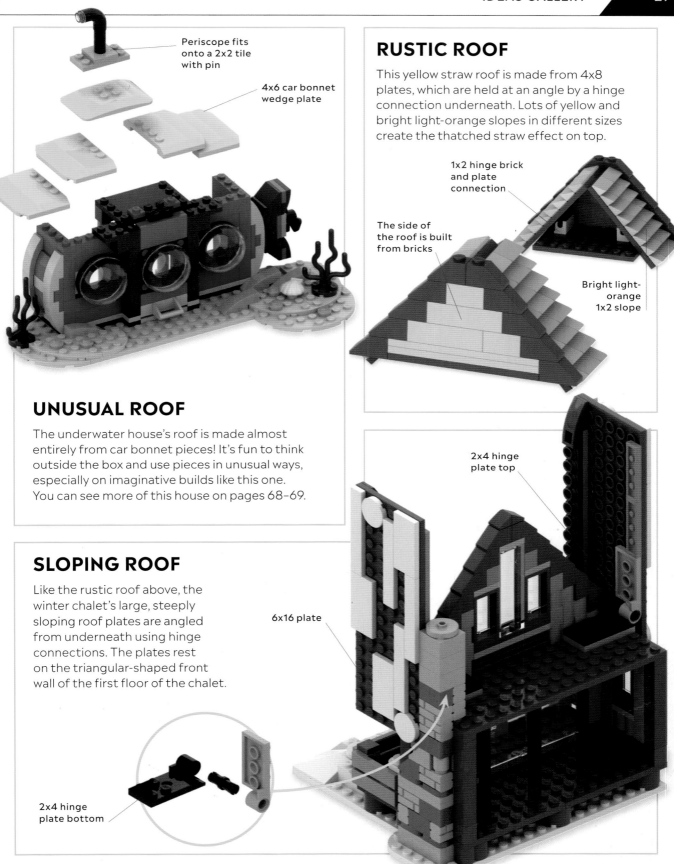

VIKING LONGHOUSE

Minifigures of the Viking Age lived in longhouses. Many Viking families lived, slept, and ate together in one big living space alongside their farm animals. This longhouse has a narrow wooden frame and a turf roof that keeps it warm in freezing temperatures.

A prophecy says this house will one day be a toy.

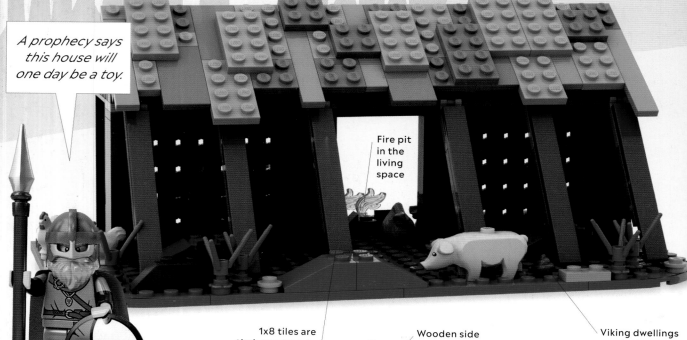

Layers of olive and lime green plates form the turf roof

Fire pit in the living space

Viking dwellings aren't the cleanest!

1x8 tiles are timber supports

Wooden side door is a 1x4x6 doorframe piece

1x1x5 bricks will be part of the front doorway

1x1x3 brick

Two 2x2 slope bricks make a turf mound

6x6 quarter round plate

LONG FRAME

A longhouse needs a long base. This one is made by combining four plate pieces. Mounds of turf cover the front half of the base, and the timber frame of the house covers the back.

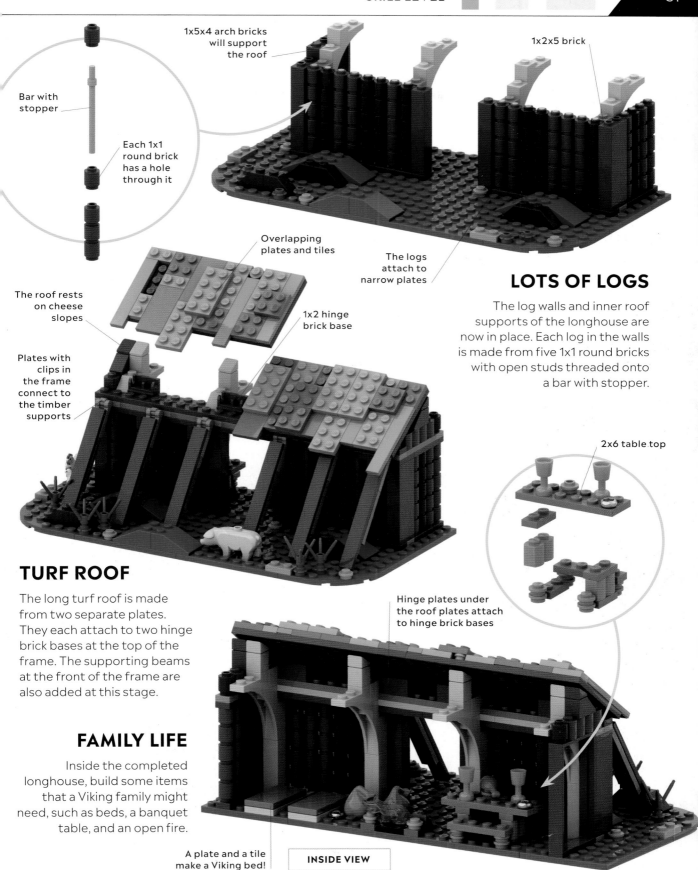

Bar with stopper

Each 1x1 round brick has a hole through it

1x5x4 arch bricks will support the roof

1x2x5 brick

Overlapping plates and tiles

The logs attach to narrow plates

LOTS OF LOGS

The log walls and inner roof supports of the longhouse are now in place. Each log in the walls is made from five 1x1 round bricks with open studs threaded onto a bar with stopper.

The roof rests on cheese slopes

Plates with clips in the frame connect to the timber supports

1x2 hinge brick base

2x6 table top

TURF ROOF

The long turf roof is made from two separate plates. They each attach to two hinge brick bases at the top of the frame. The supporting beams at the front of the frame are also added at this stage.

Hinge plates under the roof plates attach to hinge brick bases

FAMILY LIFE

Inside the completed longhouse, build some items that a Viking family might need, such as beds, a banquet table, and an open fire.

A plate and a tile make a Viking bed!

INSIDE VIEW

SKI CHALET

With a long, sloping roof and overhanging eaves, this wooden ski chalet is built in the traditional style of mountain retreats in the Alpine regions of Europe. It's a place where adventurous minifigures can enjoy warmth, comfort, and steaming hot chocolate after an exhilarating day out on the slopes.

Wheee!

White tiles are piles of snow

Floor-to-ceiling windows for taking in the views

I came here for the piste and quiet.

Build on white base plates for instant snow

Terrace lantern guides skiers home on winter nights

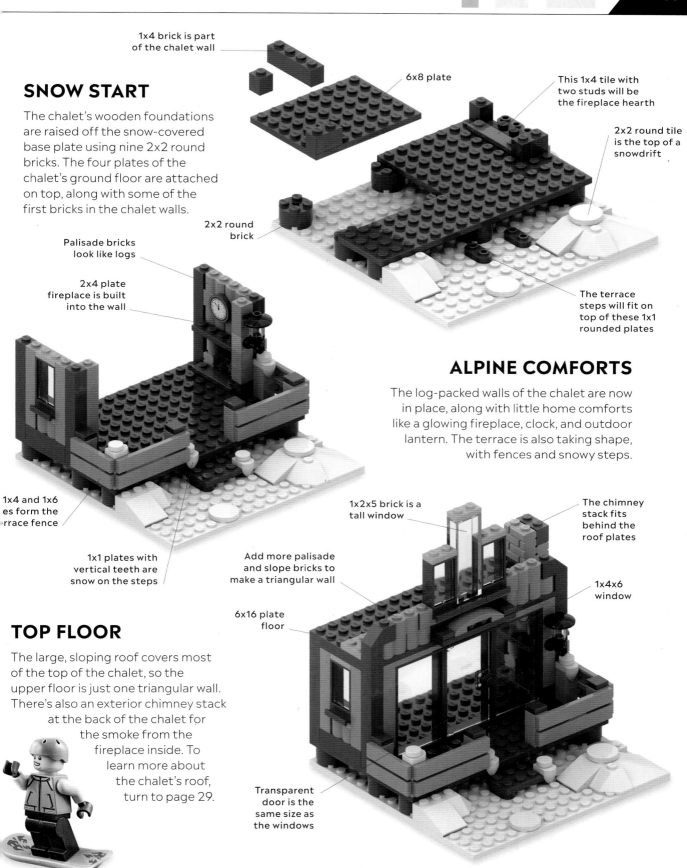

SNOW START

The chalet's wooden foundations are raised off the snow-covered base plate using nine 2x2 round bricks. The four plates of the chalet's ground floor are attached on top, along with some of the first bricks in the chalet walls.

1x4 brick is part of the chalet wall

6x8 plate

This 1x4 tile with two studs will be the fireplace hearth

2x2 round tile is the top of a snowdrift

2x2 round brick

The terrace steps will fit on top of these 1x1 rounded plates

Palisade bricks look like logs

2x4 plate fireplace is built into the wall

1x4 and 1x6 ...es form the ...rrace fence

1x1 plates with vertical teeth are snow on the steps

ALPINE COMFORTS

The log-packed walls of the chalet are now in place, along with little home comforts like a glowing fireplace, clock, and outdoor lantern. The terrace is also taking shape, with fences and snowy steps.

1x2x5 brick is a tall window

The chimney stack fits behind the roof plates

Add more palisade and slope bricks to make a triangular wall

1x4x6 window

6x16 plate floor

TOP FLOOR

The large, sloping roof covers most of the top of the chalet, so the upper floor is just one triangular wall. There's also an exterior chimney stack at the back of the chalet for the smoke from the fireplace inside. To learn more about the chalet's roof, turn to page 29.

Transparent door is the same size as the windows

BALCONIES AND TERRACES

Adding a balcony or terrace to your LEGO® house creates an extra outdoor space for your minifigures to enjoy. There are many ways to build them and many more things you could add to them, like seats, doors, or potted plants and flowers.

Romeo, Romeo... why are you a frog, Romeo?

1x3x2 inverted arch

Telescope railings

MEDIEVAL BALCONY

The balcony on the medieval inn ties in with the timber architecture of the main building. It's supported by four posts made from 1x1 round bricks. See how to build the medieval inn on pages 84–85.

CLASSIC BALCONY

Without a balcony like this, one of William Shakespeare's most famous scenes might never have happened! It is built on a plate that juts out from an upper floor, with supporting arches below.

TREEHOUSE BALCONY

Could a forest fairy or elf live behind the door of this little round balcony, built into a tree? Its pretty pearl gold railings are made from two ornamental fence pieces.

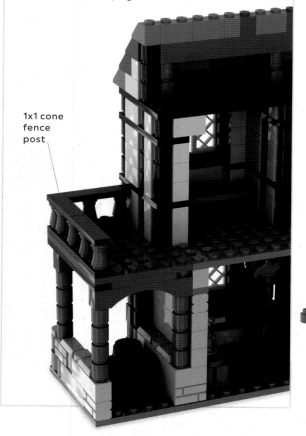

1x1 cone fence post

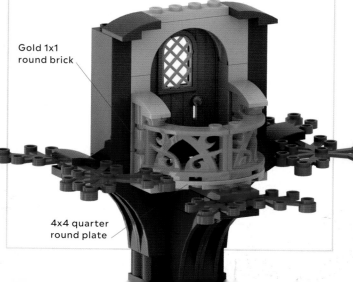

Gold 1x1 round brick

4x4 quarter round plate

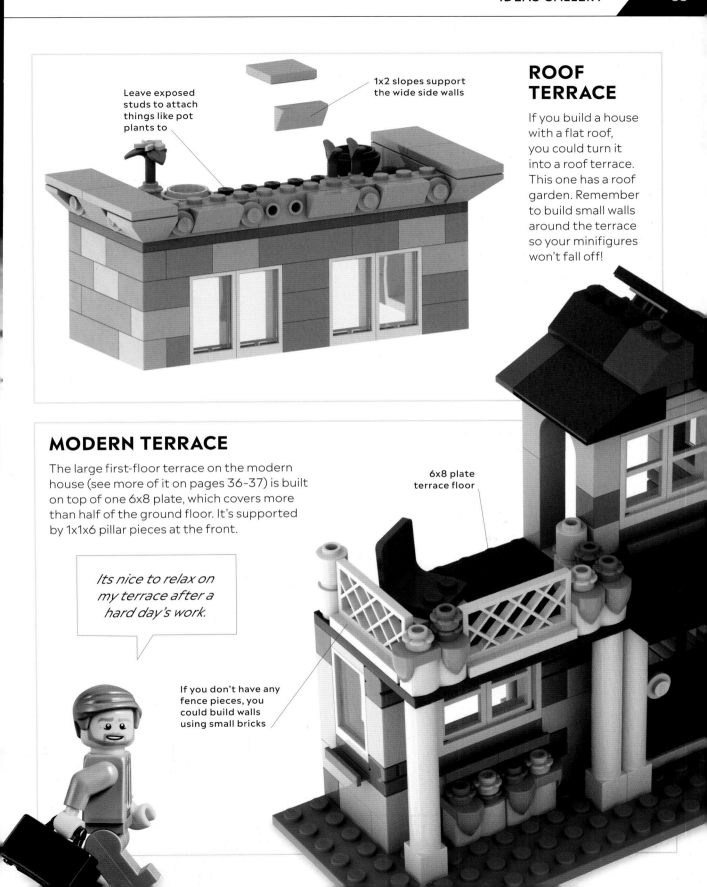

Leave exposed studs to attach things like pot plants to

1x2 slopes support the wide side walls

ROOF TERRACE

If you build a house with a flat roof, you could turn it into a roof terrace. This one has a roof garden. Remember to build small walls around the terrace so your minifigures won't fall off!

MODERN TERRACE

The large first-floor terrace on the modern house (see more of it on pages 36–37) is built on top of one 6x8 plate, which covers more than half of the ground floor. It's supported by 1x1x6 pillar pieces at the front.

Its nice to relax on my terrace after a hard day's work.

6x8 plate terrace floor

If you don't have any fence pieces, you could build walls using small bricks

MODERN HOUSE

t's no wonder this homeowner looks perfectly content in her two-storey modern home. It has solar panels that provide power and heat, sweet-scented flower boxes, and a rooftop terrace for watching the world go by.

Side windows create light-filled spaces inside

I'm sure my coffee tastes better up here.

Using different shades of green gives the plants a natural look

Vertical tooth plates make lovely hanging plants!

White column pieces support the terrace and door canopy

Palisade bricks make smart flower boxes

Build onto a green base plate to create a neatly mown lawn

The door canopy colours match the roof

TEXTURED WALLS

The modern house's walls are made from bricks in different colours and textures to give it a natural look. The white-framed windows on the front and side walls sit at the perfect height for a minifigure to peer from.

These 1x2 bricks have grooves to look like house bricks

These columns support the ground-floor ceiling

Windowsills are 1x2 plates with rails

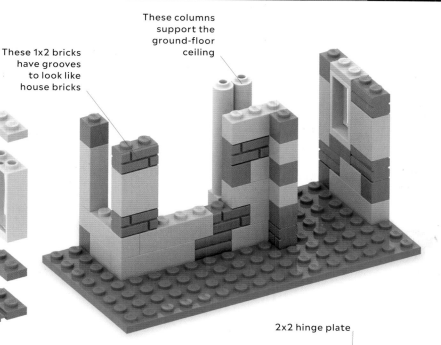

FIRST FLOOR

Two plate pieces form the ground-floor ceiling of the modern house. The walls of the first floor and the fences of the terrace are built on top of them.

1x4x2 arch brick forms the top of this doorway

Swivelling terrace chair sits on a 2x2 turntable plate

This 1x1x3 brick supports the roof

2x2 hinge plate

1x2 hinge brick base on top of a 1x2 brick

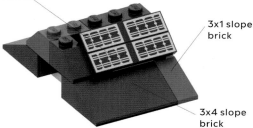

Solar panels are two printed 1x4 tiles

3x1 slope brick

3x4 slope brick

Terrace trellises made from 1x4x2 fence pieces

SOLAR-PANEL ROOF

The stepped roof can be built separately from the main home, on a 4x6 plate. The solar panels rest at an angle on the roof thanks to a hinge brick and plate connection.

SUBURBAN STREET

Treetops are 2x2 flower pieces attached upside down

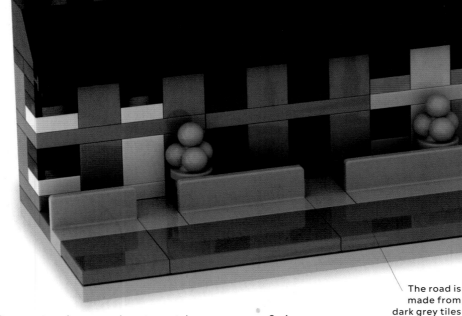

The road is made from dark grey tiles

This neat microscale street has a row of six matching houses in complementary colours. At this size, ice-cream-scoop pieces become bushes and panel pieces are garden walls. Each of the four-stud-wide houses is built separately so they can be arranged in different ways. What would your street look like in microscale?

STREET LEVEL

The base of the street is made from two long, narrow plates. They're locked together in the middle with tile pieces that will become a crossroad on the final model.

Keep your street clean!

2x4 tile fits over the seam of the plates

6x16 plate

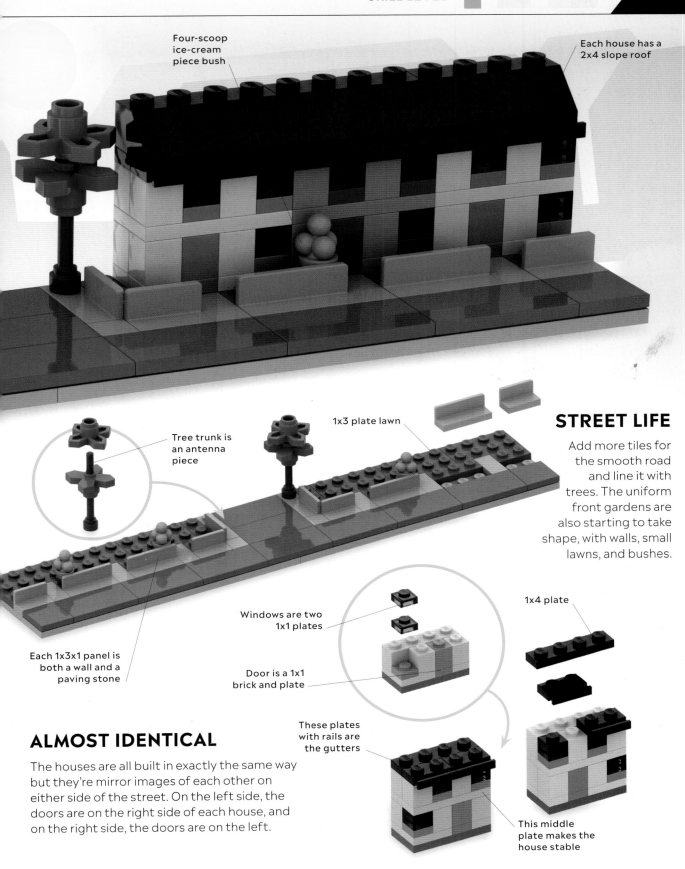

Four-scoop ice-cream piece bush

Each house has a 2x4 slope roof

STREET LIFE

Add more tiles for the smooth road and line it with trees. The uniform front gardens are also starting to take shape, with walls, small lawns, and bushes.

Tree trunk is an antenna piece

1x3 plate lawn

Each 1x3x1 panel is both a wall and a paving stone

Windows are two 1x1 plates

1x4 plate

Door is a 1x1 brick and plate

These plates with rails are the gutters

This middle plate makes the house stable

ALMOST IDENTICAL

The houses are all built in exactly the same way but they're mirror images of each other on either side of the street. On the left side, the doors are on the right side of each house, and on the right side, the doors are on the left.

TOWERS

Towers can be functional lookout points or grand-looking features that say "Look at me!" They can be connected to a main building, like a castle or a church, or stand alone, like a lighthouse or fairy-tale tower. Here are some ideas and tips for building these tall, rounded structures.

1x2 rounded plate

1x1 round brick

ROUND BUILDING

It's helpful to have rounded pieces such as macaroni bricks and arches when building round towers, but you don't need them. You can achieve a similar effect with regular bricks and plates.

CASTLE TOWER

The medieval castle has angular towers made from mostly square bricks. The only rounded pieces are the two quarter round plates that form the lookout platform at the top.

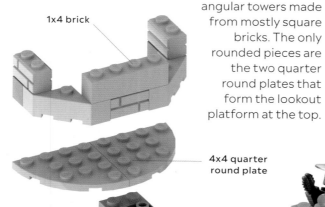

1x4 brick

4x4 quarter round plate

See more of this castle on pages 90-91

Anyone in?

LIGHTHOUSE

The lighthouse tower gets its rounded shape from stacked macaroni bricks. For stability, the tower is locked in place with round plates at regular intervals.

See how to make the top on page 21

2x2 macaroni brick

1x2 brick

4x4 quarter round plate

1x2x2 plane window

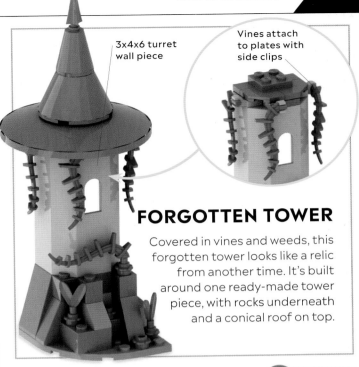

3x4x6 turret wall piece

Vines attach to plates with side clips

FORGOTTEN TOWER

Covered in vines and weeds, this forgotten tower looks like a relic from another time. It's built around one ready-made tower piece, with rocks underneath and a conical roof on top.

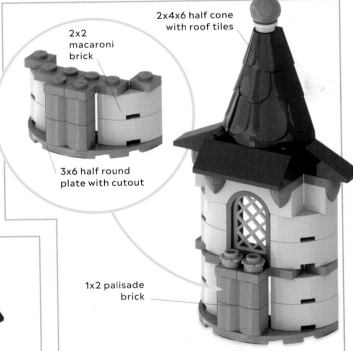

2x2 macaroni brick

3x6 half round plate with cutout

2x4x6 half cone with roof tiles

1x2 palisade brick

FAIRY-TALE TOWER

This charming build with a conical roof could be part of a fairy-tale castle or stand alone as one very tall tower. Its rounded shape is made from a combination of a half round plate, macaroni bricks, and palisade bricks.

RAINBOW HOUSE

When the sun is shining and it's raining somewhere, a rainbow appears for a little while. It looks like one such circular arc of colour has left its mark on this house, turning its roof and front lawn red and yellow and purple and green...

Small slopes form the tapered tip of the roof

2x2 slopes form the second layer of the roof

Parasol shields minifigures from the bright colours

2x2 curved slopes continue the rainbow's arc

I feel instantly at home here.

This part of the front wall is one 1x4x5 wall panel

Find out more about this seating area on page 77

COLOURFUL START

The wide walls and garden areas of the rainbow house are built on top of three green base plates in different sizes. The pillars at the back of the house will later support the brightly coloured roof.

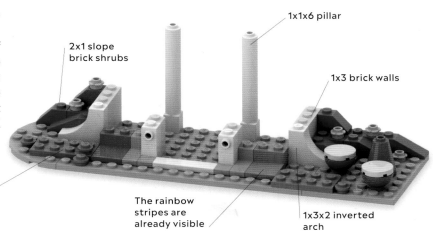

2x1 slope brick shrubs

1x1x6 pillar

1x3 brick walls

Small plates lock the base plates together

The rainbow stripes are already visible

1x3x2 inverted arch

1x3x2 arch bricks

1x2 brick with two side studs

ADDING DETAILS

Extend the rainbow stripes at the front of the house with small slopes and overhanging curved slopes, then add more of the walls and decorative doorway. The tops of the walls are made from bricks with side studs.

This brick-built doorway is wider than a regular LEGO door

Stacked 1x1 round brick column

1x6 arch brick supports the highest point of the roof

The top of the red "stripe" will fit onto this 2x2 brick

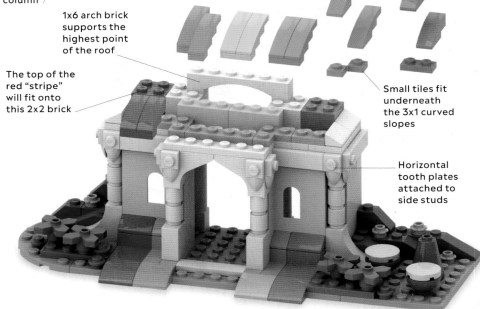

Small tiles fit underneath the 3x1 curved slopes

Horizontal tooth plates attached to side studs

RAINBOW ROOF

Once the main house is complete, it's time to begin the rainbow roof stripes. They're made from a combination of 3x1 overhanging curved slopes, slope bricks, and smaller slopes. Look back at the main picture to see the final roof build.

TOWNHOUSE

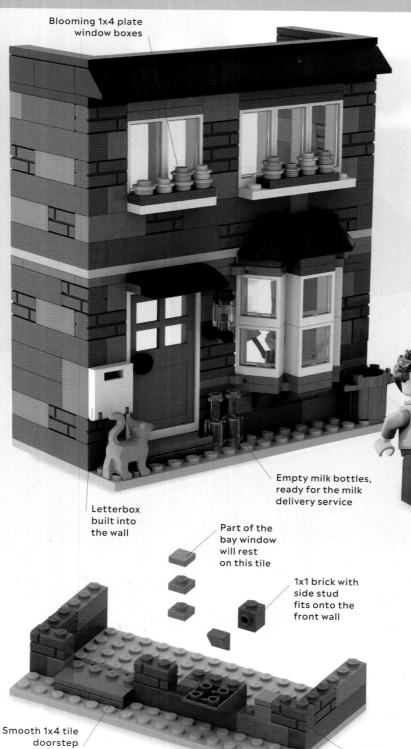

Blooming 1x4 plate window boxes

This two-storey townhouse is a home found in many towns and cities around the world. It's made from two shades of red bricks, with a wide bay window on the ground floor that lets in lots of light and provides the perfect place to relax. This home is detached, but it could also form part of a row or terrace of similar townhouses.

Empty milk bottles, ready for the milk delivery service

Letterbox built into the wall

Part of the bay window will rest on this tile

1x1 brick with side stud fits onto the front wall

Smooth 1x4 tile doorstep

1x2 dark red masonry brick

Have a good day, Colin. Can you remember to pick up a cabbage for dinner?

POLICE

HOUSE BRICKS

The townhouse covers the entire width of its 8x16 plate base. The walls are a mixture of dark red and bright red bricks – a combination that creates a natural red-brick effect. The doorstep is in place already, as is an inverted slope that will hold up the bay window.

DOWNSTAIRS

The ground floor of the townhouse now has a door, a letterbox, and a bay window. The large window is made from three separate panels, each made from two window pieces. The three window panels are held in place with hinge plates.

This 2x4 plate built into the wall will support a door canopy

Two 1x2 plates fit above this window

This 6x16 plate is the downstairs ceiling and the upstairs floor

1x2x2 window

This part of the hinge plate attaches to the wall

1x4 hinge plate

1x6 tile

This base plate is 16 studs wide, like the house

Slope bricks protrude at the front

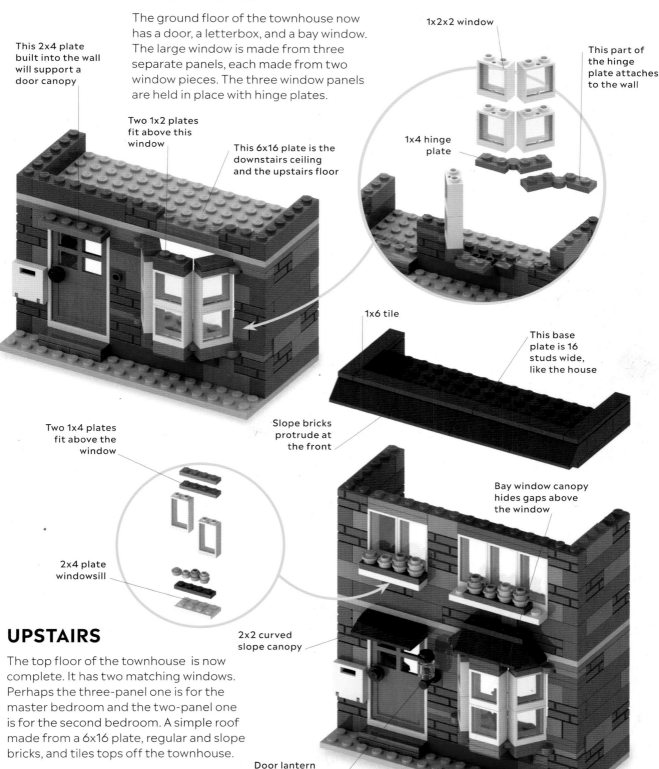

Two 1x4 plates fit above the window

2x4 plate windowsill

Bay window canopy hides gaps above the window

2x2 curved slope canopy

UPSTAIRS

The top floor of the townhouse is now complete. It has two matching windows. Perhaps the three-panel one is for the master bedroom and the two-panel one is for the second bedroom. A simple roof made from a 6x16 plate, regular and slope bricks, and tiles tops off the townhouse.

Door lantern attaches to a stud in the wall

EXTENSIONS AND EXTRAS

Once you've built a house, you might want to think about how you could extend it or add extra features. These features could be attached to the house or in the garden. Here are some ideas to extend your imagination!

> *I'd like a greenhouse, or a pool, or a garage.*

Add thriving potted plants inside

GREENHOUSE

This lean-to greenhouse is the perfect place to grow sun-loving plants because it gives them lots of light and protects them from the cold. Made from rows of window pieces, it fits snugly against the wall of a house.

Use tiles in different shapes to make an interesting path

The top of the roof leans against the wall

Small transparent pieces fill this gap

1x2 hinge brick and plates angle the roof

1x2x3 window pieces form the walls and roof

"Glass" door adds even more light

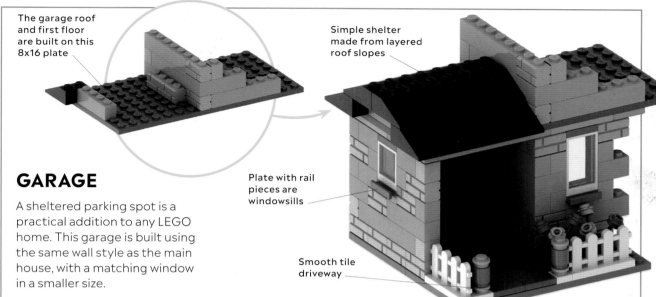

The garage roof and first floor are built on this 8x16 plate

Simple shelter made from layered roof slopes

Plate with rail pieces are windowsills

Smooth tile driveway

GARAGE

A sheltered parking spot is a practical addition to any LEGO home. This garage is built using the same wall style as the main house, with a matching window in a smaller size.

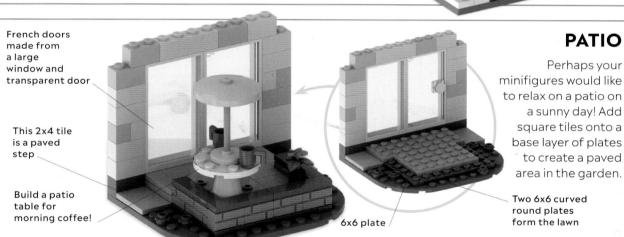

French doors made from a large window and transparent door

This 2x4 tile is a paved step

Build a patio table for morning coffee!

6x6 plate

PATIO

Perhaps your minifigures would like to relax on a patio on a sunny day! Add square tiles onto a base layer of plates to create a paved area in the garden.

Two 6x6 curved round plates form the lawn

SWIMMING POOL

Pool party! Let your minifigures live a life of luxury by building them a swimming pool. This one has glistening transparent blue water with bubbles caused by a surprise swimmer!

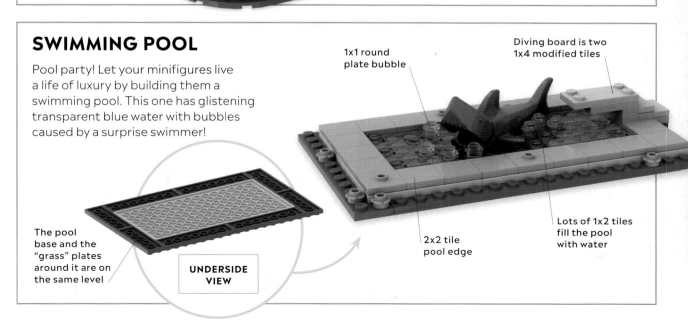

1x1 round plate bubble

Diving board is two 1x4 modified tiles

The pool base and the "grass" plates around it are on the same level

UNDERSIDE VIEW

2x2 tile pool edge

Lots of 1x2 tiles fill the pool with water

GINGERBREAD HOUSE

Vertical tooth plates make icing icicles

Candy-cane columns made from round bricks and plates

Tempting trees topped with ice-cream-scoop pieces

Plates with rails work well as small windowsills

This caramel-latticed door pane matches the windows

Pink-iced fence posts are 1x1 round plates with swirled tops

With its winding cookie path, candy-cane doorway, and frosted icing roof, this little home looks good enough to eat. But don't try that, or you might need a trip to the dentist – and it won't be because you ate too many sweets!

We just brought our baby home from the bakery!

"Caramel" 1x1 round plate

1x1 tile with cookie pattern

2x2 corner slope

Leave space for the windows

GINGERBREAD BEGINNINGS

Place cookie-patterned 1x1 tiles on a 16x16 base plate to form the garden path. Then create the iced outline of the house and start building the gingerbread and caramel walls.

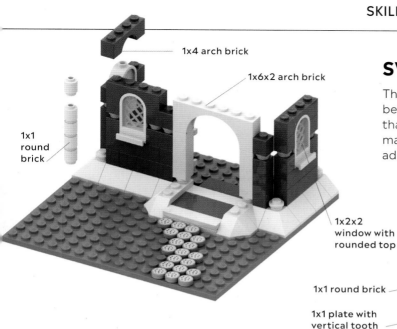

1x4 arch brick

1x6x2 arch brick

1x1 round brick

1x2x2 window with rounded top

SWEET DETAILS

The walls of a real gingerbread house would be joined at the corners with icing. Create that look by adding white corner columns made from stacked 1x1 round bricks. Then add the doorframe arches and windows.

The roof will rest on these 1x1 slopes

1x2 hinge brick

1x1 round brick

1x1 plate with vertical tooth

DELICIOUS DOORWAY

Use a 4x6 plate to make the doorway canopy and add icing icicles and round tiles in the bright colours of boiled sweets. There are now smaller plates and slopes on top of the walls – these will support the house's upper wall and roof.

Bar with stopper

1x1 plate with vertical tooth

1x1 round tile with swirl pattern

1x2/1x2 bracket

Small slope pieces give this wall a tapered shape

ICED ROOF

The gingerbread roof is made in two parts that rest on the tapered top wall of the house. Both roof pieces are made from brown 6x10 plates trimmed with white brackets and vertical tooth plates to look like perfectly piped icing.

MODULAR APARTMENTS

I think I'll build my apartment right on top.

In bustling towns and cities, many people live in apartment blocks like this one. The two separate, open-plan flats in this block are stacked on top of each other, but they can also be joined at the side – this makes them modular builds. You could build even more flats to make a tower block!

Details like this air-conditioning unit bring the building to life

The top-floor flat has a roof terrace

Modern balcony railing made from window panels on their sides

Oh no, I can't ride it. It just looks cool!

Apartment letterboxes on the ground floor

Neat floor made from tiles

Other apartment blocks could be attached here using LEGO® Technic pins

BOTTOM UP

Each modular apartment is built on a square 16x16 plate, with walls made from a mixture of plain and textured masonry bricks. The ground-floor apartment has a tiled front entrance with letterboxes built into the wall.

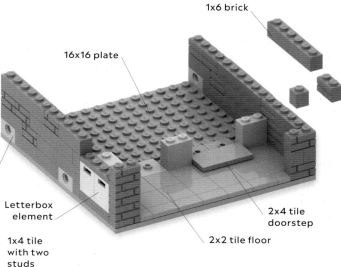

1x6 brick

16x16 plate

1x2 brick with hole

Letterbox element

1x4 tile with two studs

2x4 tile doorstep

2x2 tile floor

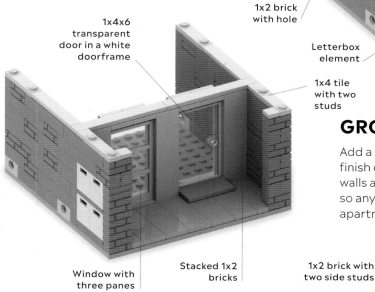

1x4x6 transparent door in a white doorframe

Window with three panes

Stacked 1x2 bricks

GROUND FLOOR

Add a modern door and window and finish off the walls. The tops of the walls are lined with mostly smooth tiles, so any floors that are added above the apartment can easily be lifted off.

2x2 printed tile

1x4 brick side walls

1x2 brick with two side studs

1x4 brick with side studs

1x2 grille tile

1x8 plate with rail

1x1 round elbow brick

1x8 tile

ROOF

This square roof could be added to any number of modular apartments. Like the apartments, it's built on a 16x16 base plate. Add low walls around its sides to make it a roof terrace, and add practical details like pipes and air-conditioning units.

1x6 tile

Stacked 1x1 round plates with three leaves

UPPER FLOOR

The second floor of the modular apartment block is built in the same way as the ground-floor apartment, except it has a balcony with railings, and a pot plant in place of letterboxes.

2x2 inverted dome pot

1x2x3 window

MICROSCALE MODELS

Your houses, gardens, and streets don't have to be built for minifigures. At microscale, which is any size smaller than minifigure scale, the tiniest pieces can become whole objects. Think of something big and work out how to build it small, then build anything else in your model at the same scale so everything looks in proportion.

Plate with side clip is a bus stop sign

STREET FURNITURE

This whole street scene, featuring a potted bush, a bench, a bus stop, and a waste bin, fits onto one 2x8 base plate. The 1x8 tile at the front is the smooth road surface.

SUBURBAN STREET

Each of this microscale street's houses is only four studs wide. They're all built on a 2x4 base plate, with doors and windows made from small bricks and plates.

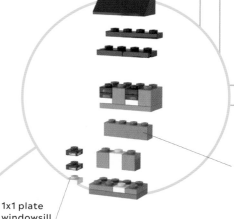

One 1x4 brick covers the back of the ground floor

Plates with rails under the roofs are the gutters

1x1 plate windowsill

You could also make mini vehicles to go on the mini road

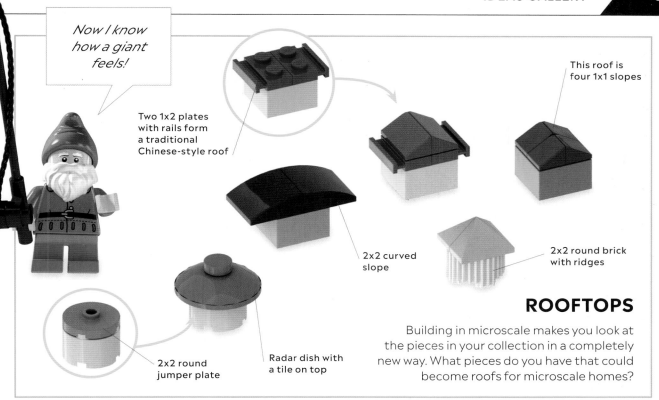

Now I know how a giant feels!

Two 1x2 plates with rails form a traditional Chinese-style roof

This roof is four 1x1 slopes

2x2 curved slope

2x2 round brick with ridges

2x2 round jumper plate

Radar dish with a tile on top

ROOFTOPS

Building in microscale makes you look at the pieces in your collection in a completely new way. What pieces do you have that could become roofs for microscale homes?

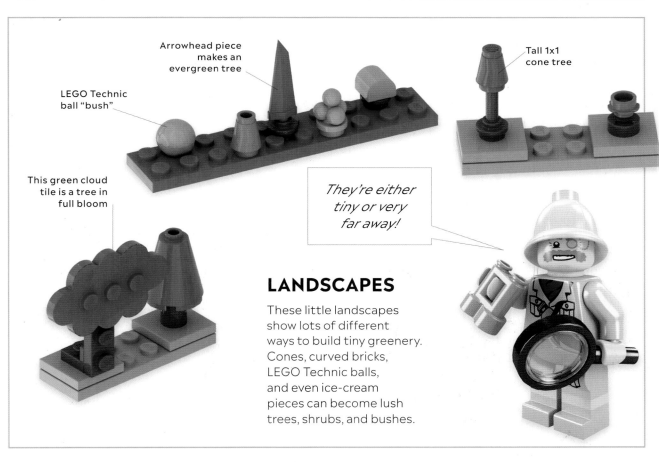

Arrowhead piece makes an evergreen tree

Tall 1x1 cone tree

LEGO Technic ball "bush"

This green cloud tile is a tree in full bloom

They're either tiny or very far away!

LANDSCAPES

These little landscapes show lots of different ways to build tiny greenery. Cones, curved bricks, LEGO Technic balls, and even ice-cream pieces can become lush trees, shrubs, and bushes.

HILLSIDE VILLAGE

This should be easy enough to invade.

When building in microscale, you can literally have a whole world in your hands. This entire hilltop village – with leafy greenery, buildings of all shapes and sizes, and a gently winding road running through it – fits onto one 8x16 base plate.

Church made from 1x1 bricks and slopes

Trees made from 1x1 cones and bar pieces

1x1 double curved slope roof

1x4 palisade bricks add interesting texture

Bricks on the edge will be seen, so they're grey

This 1x8 plate won't be seen later

8x16 base plate

2x4 round plate

GOING UPHILL

To begin the gently sloping hill, add bricks at the back, where the highest part of the hill will be, and plates at the front. As most of the pieces on the bottom layer won't be seen, they can be any colour you like.

STEEP CLIMB

Now there are more bricks and plates on the hillside, in natural-looking greys, browns, and greens. The dark grey winding road is also starting to take shape. Two 10x1 curved slopes form the steepest parts of the road.

1x2 rounded plate

Bricks at the back add height

This is the highest point of the hill

These 1x1 cones will become a cluster of bushes

2x2 macaroni tile

LUSH LANDSCAPE

Complete the winding road with curved tiles, then add more greenery to the hillside using cones for bushes and round plates for tree-trunk bases. The grey round plates are rocky parts of the hillside.

This 1x4 tile is the only flat, straight part of the road

1x1 round plate rock

Build houses at different heights by using a mixture of plates and bricks

The bar piece trunk fits into this cone

You build it, I knock it down.

Stacked 1x1 bricks are the church spire

VILLAGE LIFE

Last come the buildings that bring the hillside village to life. Use some of the tiniest bricks you have, such as 1x1 bricks and cheese slopes, to create all kinds of homes and functional buildings.

1x1 double curved slopes make rounded roofs

PLAYHOUSE

This is one *fun* house! No one lives in this colourful wooden structure, but plenty of children visit it every day to play. There's a climbing wall, a tyre swing, a spiral slide to whizz down, and plenty of cosy corners to play house or hide-and-seek in.

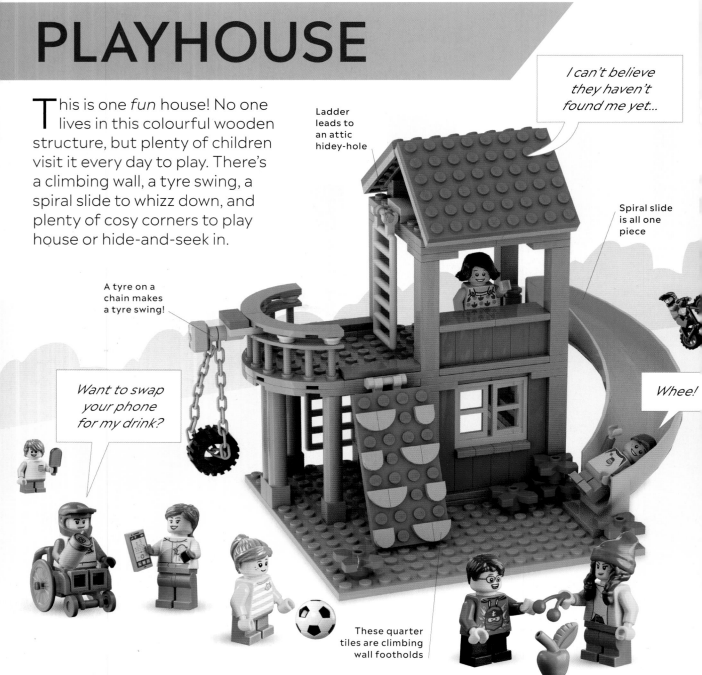

Ladder leads to an attic hidey-hole

I can't believe they haven't found me yet...

Spiral slide is all one piece

A tyre on a chain makes a tyre swing!

Want to swap your phone for my drink?

Whee!

These quarter tiles are climbing wall footholds

LET'S PLAY

The playhouse has a wooden base of nougat brown plates topped with tiles around the edges. The blue panels on the wall are 1x2 tiles attached sideways to studs in the wall. The house fits neatly in the corner of a 16x16 plate.

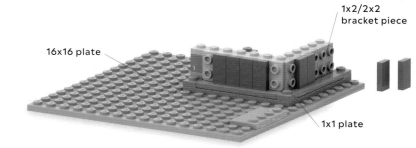

1x2/2x2 bracket piece

16x16 plate

1x1 plate

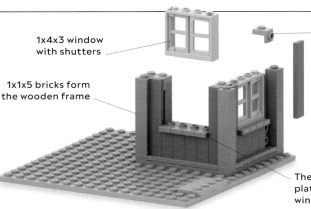

1x4x3 window with shutters

1x1/1x1 bracket holds up the longer 1x6 tile

1x1x5 bricks form the wooden frame

These four jumper plates are the windowsill

PEEKABOO

Build up the wall by adding more blue panels and a wooden frame. Then add wide windows with shutters for children to peek out from.

8x8 plate with rounded end

1x1x6 pillar

SUPPORTING PILLARS

Once the main house is finished, add pillars and a tall brick to support a wide first floor. A square 8x8 plate fits onto studs on top of the house's walls.

2x2 plate

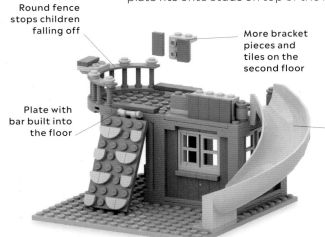

Round fence stops children falling off

More bracket pieces and tiles on the second floor

Plate with bar built into the floor

If you don't have a slide piece, you could build your own

6x8 plate roof slope

1x2 hinge plate connects the roof to the house

1x2 hinge brick base

SLIDE AND CLIMB

Now this house is starting to look much more fun, with its slide and climbing wall in place. The slide attaches to the 8x8 plate on the first floor, while the wall hangs from a clip-and-bar connection.

Climb the step ladder to get in

4x4 macaroni tiles top off the fence

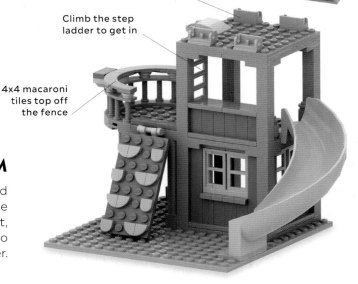

ATTIC ROOM

Finish off the playhouse by building a third floor. First, build a second wooden frame and place another 8x8 plate on top. Next, attach sloping roof plates to this floor to make a snug attic room with a step ladder.

GARDEN PLANTS

No matter how big or small a LEGO home's garden is, adding plants and flowers will really bring it to life. Gardens can be neat or overgrown, and full of colourful flowers, rows of vegetables, or wild weeds! The choice of colours you use can even reflect the season. Animals enjoy gardens as much as minifigures do, so you could add some of those, too.

AUTUMN TREE

Make an autumnal tree by adding leaves or other pieces in autumnal colours. Leaving the tree's branches bare changes the season to winter.

Mushrooms also appear in autumn

SHRUBBERY

Short plants with lots of stems are called shrubs. When lots of shrubs are planted together like this, they are shrubbery. You can make your own by stacking up lots of similar leaf pieces in small sections.

Add flowers (or chickens!) for extra detail

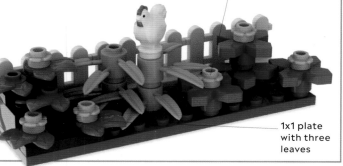

1x1 plate with three leaves

You can't "beet" vegetables!

VEGETABLE PATCH

Help your minifigures to "grow their own" by building them a vegetable garden. This flourishing plot features neat rows of carrots, leeks, and other vegetables surrounded by soil.

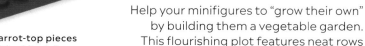

Carrot-top pieces with white 1x1 plates are leeks

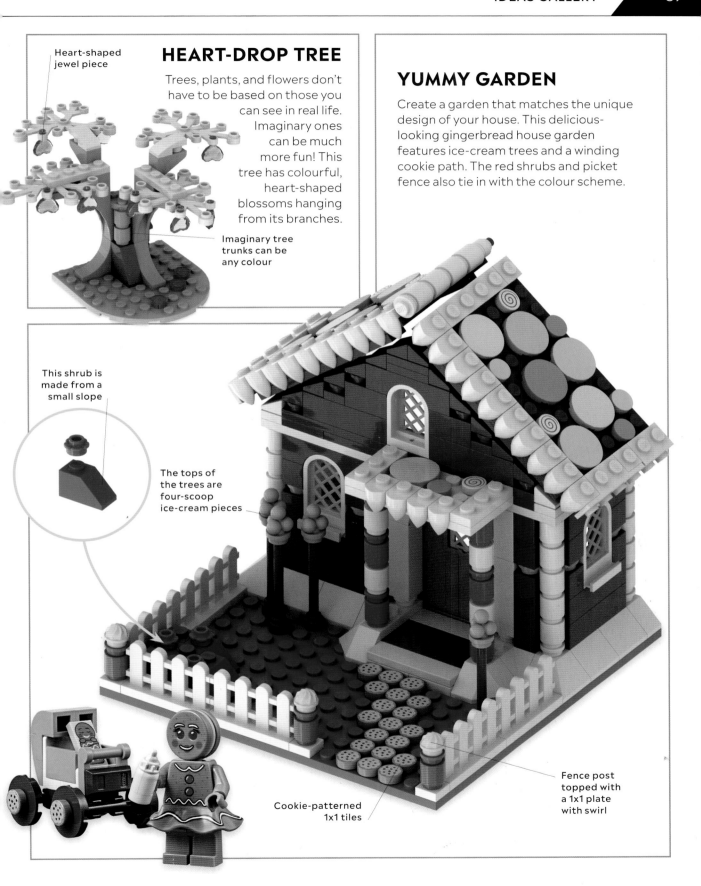

HEART-DROP TREE

Trees, plants, and flowers don't have to be based on those you can see in real life. Imaginary ones can be much more fun! This tree has colourful, heart-shaped blossoms hanging from its branches.

Heart-shaped jewel piece

Imaginary tree trunks can be any colour

YUMMY GARDEN

Create a garden that matches the unique design of your house. This delicious-looking gingerbread house garden features ice-cream trees and a winding cookie path. The red shrubs and picket fence also tie in with the colour scheme.

This shrub is made from a small slope

The tops of the trees are four-scoop ice-cream pieces

Fence post topped with a 1x1 plate with swirl

Cookie-patterned 1x1 tiles

SNAIL HOUSE

There are no limits to the kinds of houses you can build in LEGO® bricks – as this imaginative home proves! A shell is a snail's house, so why can't it be a minifigure's, too? Its bright pink shell has latticed windows and a letterbox for any snail mail.

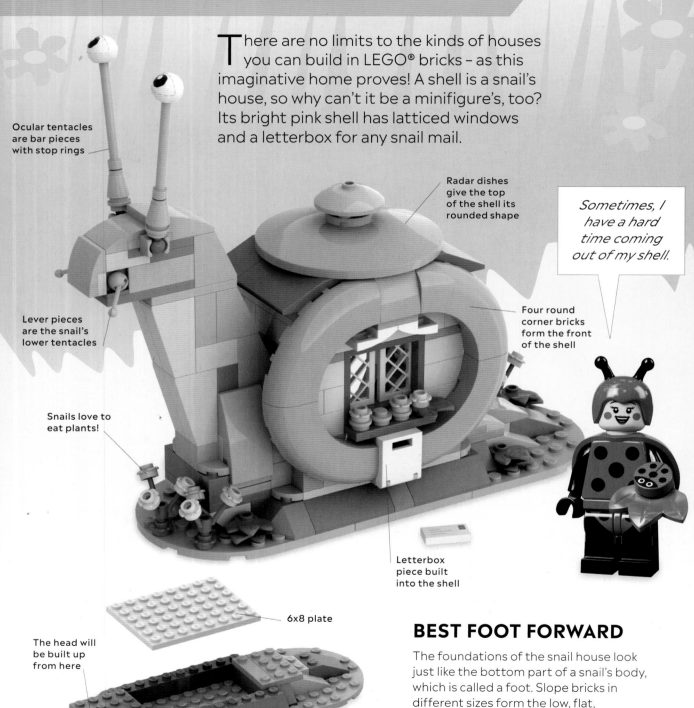

Ocular tentacles are bar pieces with stop rings

Radar dishes give the top of the shell its rounded shape

Sometimes, I have a hard time coming out of my shell.

Lever pieces are the snail's lower tentacles

Four round corner bricks form the front of the shell

Snails love to eat plants!

Letterbox piece built into the shell

6x8 plate

The head will be built up from here

2x4 slope brick

BEST FOOT FORWARD

The foundations of the snail house look just like the bottom part of a snail's body, which is called a foot. Slope bricks in different sizes form the low, flat, slithering shape. The 6x8 plate that fits on top of the foot section will become the floor of the house.

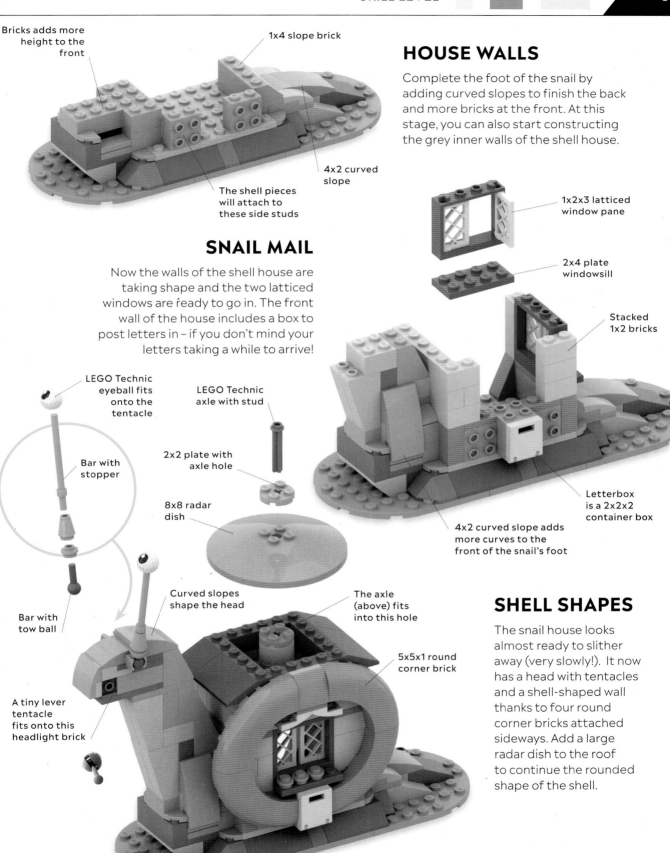

Bricks adds more height to the front

1x4 slope brick

The shell pieces will attach to these side studs

4x2 curved slope

HOUSE WALLS

Complete the foot of the snail by adding curved slopes to finish the back and more bricks at the front. At this stage, you can also start constructing the grey inner walls of the shell house.

1x2x3 latticed window pane

2x4 plate windowsill

SNAIL MAIL

Now the walls of the shell house are taking shape and the two latticed windows are ready to go in. The front wall of the house includes a box to post letters in – if you don't mind your letters taking a while to arrive!

Stacked 1x2 bricks

Letterbox is a 2x2x2 container box

4x2 curved slope adds more curves to the front of the snail's foot

LEGO Technic eyeball fits onto the tentacle

LEGO Technic axle with stud

Bar with stopper

2x2 plate with axle hole

8x8 radar dish

Bar with tow ball

Curved slopes shape the head

The axle (above) fits into this hole

5x5x1 round corner brick

A tiny lever tentacle fits onto this headlight brick

SHELL SHAPES

The snail house looks almost ready to slither away (very slowly!). It now has a head with tentacles and a shell-shaped wall thanks to four round corner bricks attached sideways. Add a large radar dish to the roof to continue the rounded shape of the shell.

THATCHED COTTAGE

This cosy countryside cottage looks like it could have been home to minifigures for hundreds of years. It has a thatched roof, which means it is made from layers of straw or other dried plants, and uneven grey walls that have stood the test of time.

1x2 grille plates look like stalks of straw

Round tiles attach to side studs in the walls

Uneven garden path made from round tiles in different sizes

This rabbit likes the wild country garden

These green round plates with petals could be small plants or moss

I hope grandma will be home.

2x4 tile doorstep

Colourful 1x1 round-plate flowers in the window box

HUMBLE BEGINNINGS

The walls of the thatched cottage are made from a variety of grey bricks. Using pieces in different shades, shapes, and sizes gives the walls a weathered look. An open fire on the cottage floor heats the home.

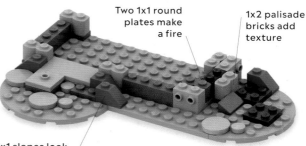

Two 1x1 round plates make a fire

1x2 palisade bricks add texture

2x1 slopes look like overgrown grass

HOMELY DETAILS

Now there are window boxes, and a mantelpiece over the cosy fire. The quirky shape of the chimney is built up using a mixture of round bricks, palisade bricks, and bricks with side studs.

1x2 jumper plate

1x1 round brick

1x4 plate mantelpiece

1x1 brick with side stud

1x2 slope

1x4 brick with side studs

2x2 round brick

Telescope piece

1x1 brick with side clip

WALL FINISHES

Arch bricks fit into the walls above the wood-framed latticed windows and doors. There are lots of exposed side studs in the wall bricks so other pieces can attach to them later. There's also a brick with clip facing inside that has an old-fashioned torch attached to it.

1x2 grille plates fit onto the two lower plates

2x2 hinge plate attaches to the lowest of the three roof plates

1x2 hinge bricks attach to plates above the walls

2x12 plate

1x6 arch

CRAFTING THE THATCH

The sides of the thatched roof are made from various slope pieces that stack up on top of the walls. The front and back of it are separate pieces built from overlapping layers of 2x12 plates. They attach to the main house with hinge brick and plate connections.

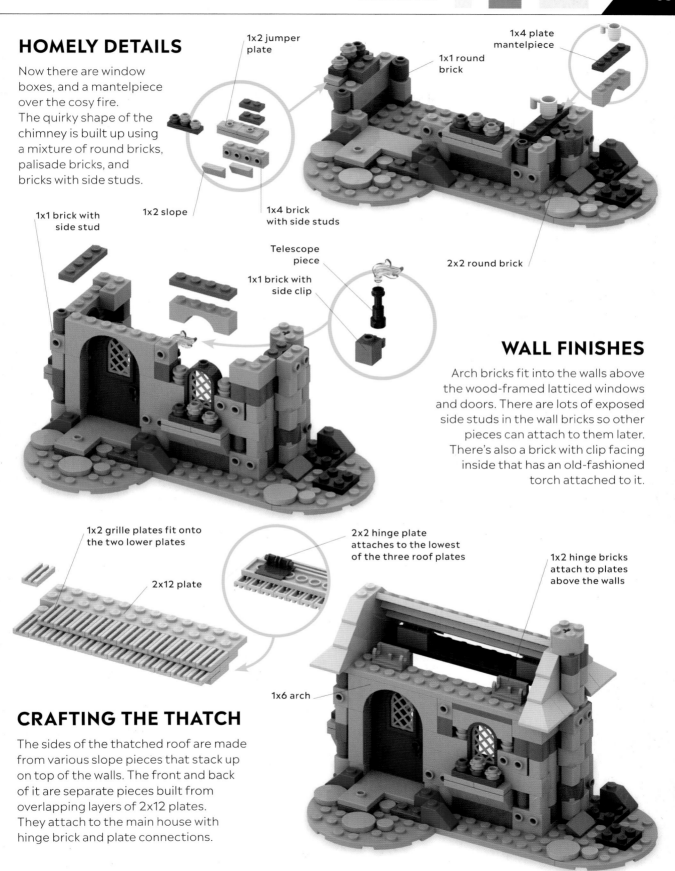

UNUSUAL FEATURES

Let your imagination run wild and build some unusual, funny, or functional features for your LEGO houses. Think about where your house is located, who lives in it, and what they might need to live and laugh there.

You can see more of this house on pages 72–73

Axle pin connector

The periscope can rotate on this pin

UNDER THE SEA

The underwater house has lots of submarine features, such as a propeller and rudder for moving through water. It also has a rotating periscope for peering above the surface. See how to build this house on pages 68–69.

Macaroni tube

Small propeller attaches to a tile with pin

Large wings attach to clips in the houses's walls

The house attaches to 2x2 jumper plates

3x5 cloud tile

Bird, house, plane... what's not to love?

UP IN THE CLOUDS

Can you imagine living in a house with wings? Where would you fly to? The flying house's wings flap up and down on clip-and-bar connections. It has a cloud perch to come home to roost on.

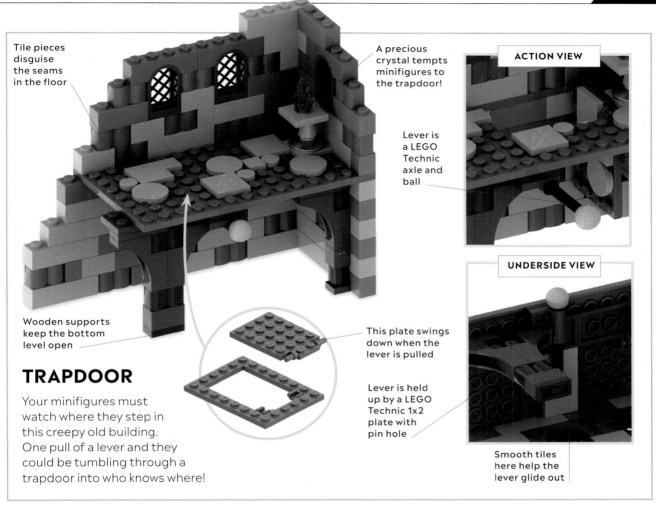

Tile pieces disguise the seams in the floor

A precious crystal tempts minifigures to the trapdoor!

ACTION VIEW

Lever is a LEGO Technic axle and ball

Wooden supports keep the bottom level open

TRAPDOOR

Your minifigures must watch where they step in this creepy old building. One pull of a lever and they could be tumbling through a trapdoor into who knows where!

This plate swings down when the lever is pulled

Lever is held up by a LEGO Technic 1x2 plate with pin hole

UNDERSIDE VIEW

Smooth tiles here help the lever glide out

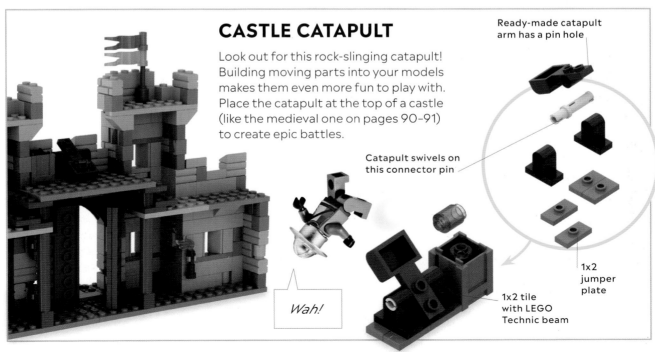

CASTLE CATAPULT

Look out for this rock-slinging catapult! Building moving parts into your models makes them even more fun to play with. Place the catapult at the top of a castle (like the medieval one on pages 90–91) to create epic battles.

Ready-made catapult arm has a pin hole

Catapult swivels on this connector pin

Wah!

1x2 tile with LEGO Technic beam

1x2 jumper plate

HAMBURGER HOUSE

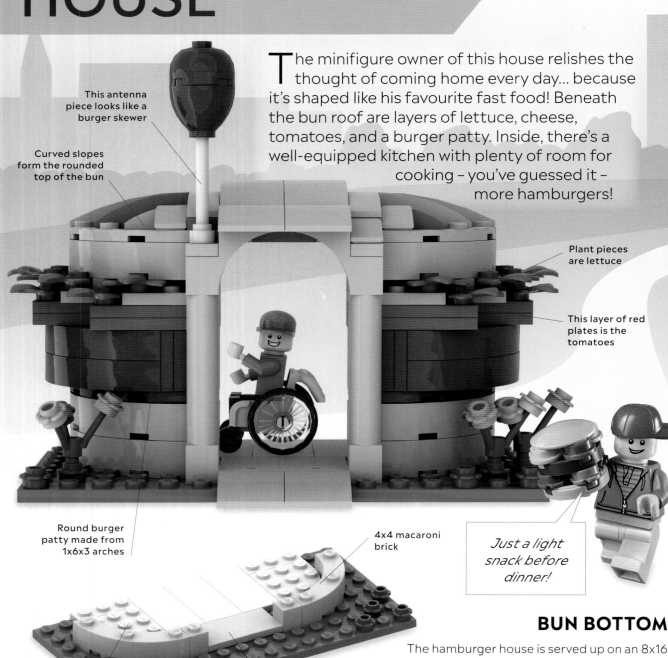

The minifigure owner of this house relishes the thought of coming home every day... because it's shaped like his favourite fast food! Beneath the bun roof are layers of lettuce, cheese, tomatoes, and a burger patty. Inside, there's a well-equipped kitchen with plenty of room for cooking – you've guessed it – more hamburgers!

This antenna piece looks like a burger skewer

Curved slopes form the rounded top of the bun

Plant pieces are lettuce

This layer of red plates is the tomatoes

Round burger patty made from 1x6x3 arches

4x4 macaroni brick

Kitchen equipment will fit onto these studs later

2x4 tile for the doorway

Just a light snack before dinner!

BUN BOTTOM

The hamburger house is served up on an 8x16 base plate. To begin its bun-shaped foundations, attach large macaroni bricks for the house's walls, a 2x4 tile for the doorway opening, and white plates and tiles for the kitchen floor.

I think I've eaten too much.

BUILD A BURGER

Add more macaroni and other bricks to build up the beige bun, then begin the burger build, starting with macaroni tiles. At the back, build in some arch bricks that will later support the bun lid roof. It's a good idea to think about ways to make your model stable at the early stages of building, so it's easy to play with later.

See more of this kitchen equipment on page 82

1x3x3 arch brick

Tap pieces are ketchup and mustard

4x4 macaroni tile

This doorframe with pillars is all one piece

2x3 plate cheese slice

Round 1x1 plate with three leaves

NO GHERKINS?

Once the burger patty is in place, it's time to add the relish. Layer up red-plate tomatoes and yellow-plate cheese, then add plant pieces as lettuce leaves. You could add any relishes you like to your hamburger house. What will you choose?

2x2 curved slopes make the door ramp

Two plates are shorter than a brick

2x6 plate

UNDER THE BUN LID

Beneath the curved slopes of the bun lid are plates and bricks in various shapes and sizes. They bring together two 6x6 corner plates and build up the height of the bun so it's taller in the middle.

Taller bricks in the middle of the bun

6x6 corner plate

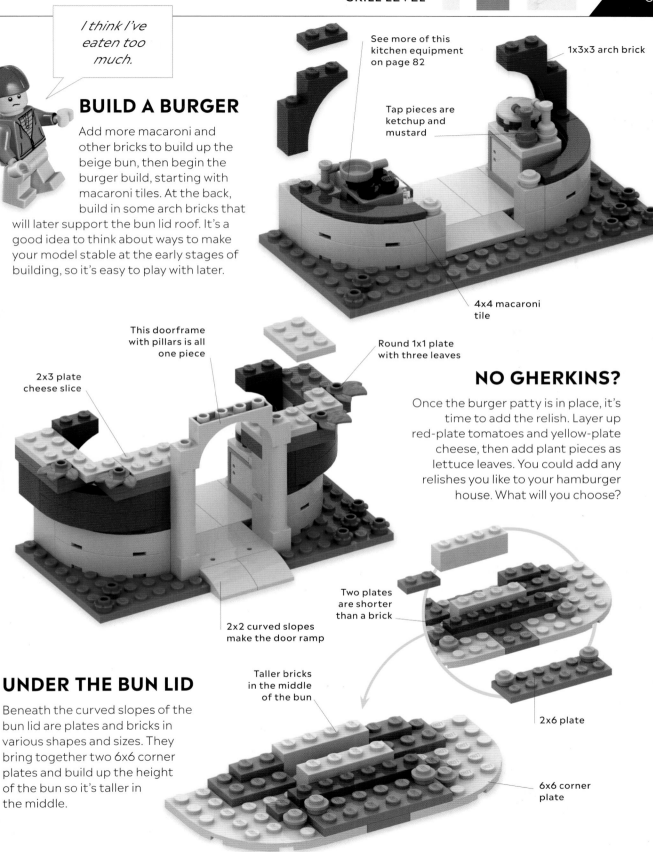

UNDERWATER HOUSE

This aquatic home is located in the dark depths of the ocean, on the seabed. All kinds of marine life whizz past its three bubble windows, wondering what on earth it is. Half-submarine, half-home, the underwater house has a rudder and propeller so it can relocate in a flash if any predators approach.

The home's residents can peer out of this periscope

These pieces are more often used as car bonnets

Small propeller spins on a tile with pin

The front door opens from the bottom

Watertight bubble window attaches to a 4x4 round plate with hole

1x1x6 pillars support the roof but leave the back of the house open

1x4 brick wall

1x2 tile doorstep

Layered round tiles create a ripple effect

SANDY START

The curvy, uneven base of the underwater house looks like ripples of sand on the seabed. It's made from one rectangular 8x16 plate surrounded by round plates in different sizes. Plates form the lowest parts of the house's walls, with a layer of bricks on top.

SUBMARINE SIDES

The walls of the underwater house are deceiving – they look round but they're actually square! Each square wall contains a brick with four side studs so that separate, rounded walls can be attached sideways.

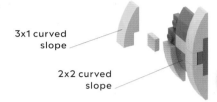

3x1 curved slope

2x2 curved slope

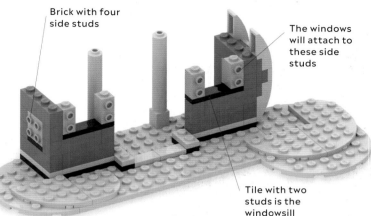

Brick with four side studs

The windows will attach to these side studs

Tile with two studs is the windowsill

4x4 round plate with 2x2 hole

4x4 cylinder

BUBBLE WINDOWS

A house underwater needs big bubble windows! These ones are made from cylinders attached to round plates with holes. They fit onto bricks with side studs on either side of the window openings in the wall.

The roof will rest on this 1x1 brick

Stacked 1x2 bricks create an extra-thick doorframe

WATERTIGHT DOOR

The heavy, submarine-style door has a matching bubble window. It opens from the handle at the bottom and hangs from a plate with bar built into the roof.

Learn more about the unusual roof on page 29

The door clips onto this plate with bar

Add tiles to make the door look heavier and more watertight

1x2 plate with two clips

REAR VIEW

Door handle is a 2x1 tile with bar

Cylinder is the same size as the other windows

TIME TO PLAY

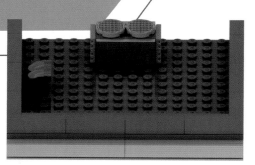

Just eight studs hold the roof in place

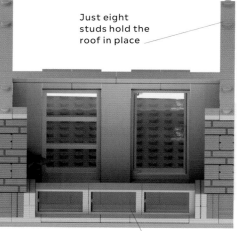

While you're thinking about ways to make your LEGO house look good on the outside, you might also want to consider how you can access it to play on the inside. In Danish, "LEGO" means "play well" – making your models easy to play with helps you to do just that.

See how to make this roof on pages 6-7

The whole roof and chimney section lifts off

The door is a more fiddly access point!

Modified 1x4 tile with two studs

The balcony is another place to play

OPEN SIDES

The modular apartment (pages 50–51) has a roof that can easily be removed. The apartment is also open on two sides – on the balcony and at the back – to make access even easier.

RAISING THE ROOF

Playing inside the simple house is really simple – just lift off the roof. It attaches to four studs at the top of the main house. The rest of the top layer of the house is made from smooth tiles.

HIDDEN OPENING

You could build hidden hinges into one of your house's walls for a more surprising way to open it up. The whole wall – including any windows and pretty flower boxes – would then open like a door. Perhaps a secret meeting could be taking place inside…

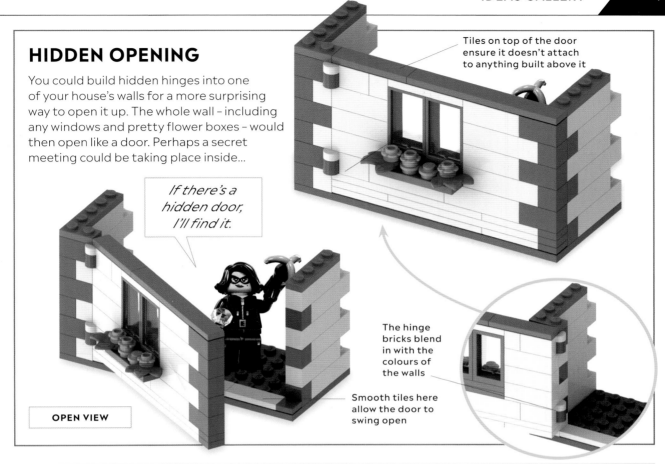

Tiles on top of the door ensure it doesn't attach to anything built above it

If there's a hidden door, I'll find it.

The hinge bricks blend in with the colours of the walls

OPEN VIEW

Smooth tiles here allow the door to swing open

SPLIT HOUSE

The country cottage has hinge pieces inside its chimney stack so the whole house can split in half and open up like a storybook. Now there's room to create endless stories inside as well as outside.

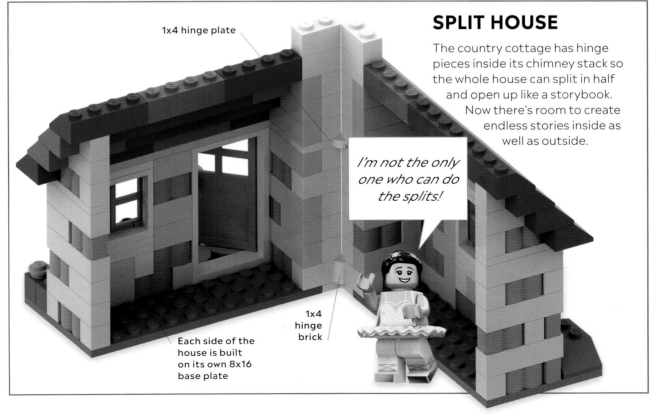

1x4 hinge plate

I'm not the only one who can do the splits!

1x4 hinge brick

Each side of the house is built on its own 8x16 base plate

FLYING HOUSE

Who wants to live in a street when you can live high up in the clouds? This bird-shaped house with brightly coloured plumage is not only a delightful imaginary home – it's also a form of transportation. It can take off from its cloud perch and soar through the skies.

And they say I'm make-believe!

Arch bricks are pink tail feathers

Large, flapping wings

Curved bricks in different sizes make fluffy clouds

Curved-slope beak

Horn pieces make sharp talons

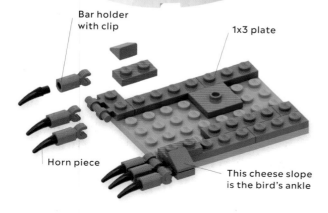

Bar holder with clip

1x3 plate

Horn piece

This cheese slope is the bird's ankle

FEET FIRST

Begin this bird-like build with a 6x8 plate, adding narrow plates for the bases of the side walls. Next, make the bird's feet and claws. Start with a 1x2 plate with bar handle and clip three bar holders to it. Add horn pieces to create the talons.

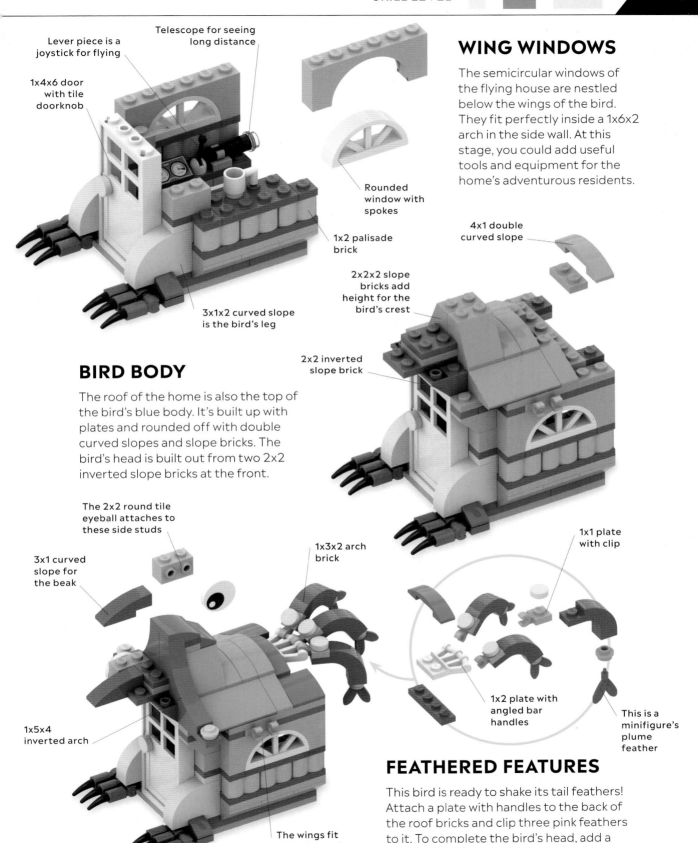

Lever piece is a joystick for flying

Telescope for seeing long distance

1x4x6 door with tile doorknob

WING WINDOWS

The semicircular windows of the flying house are nestled below the wings of the bird. They fit perfectly inside a 1x6x2 arch in the side wall. At this stage, you could add useful tools and equipment for the home's adventurous residents.

Rounded window with spokes

1x2 palisade brick

4x1 double curved slope

3x1x2 curved slope is the bird's leg

2x2x2 slope bricks add height for the bird's crest

2x2 inverted slope brick

BIRD BODY

The roof of the home is also the top of the bird's blue body. It's built up with plates and rounded off with double curved slopes and slope bricks. The bird's head is built out from two 2x2 inverted slope bricks at the front.

The 2x2 round tile eyeball attaches to these side studs

3x1 curved slope for the beak

1x3x2 arch brick

1x1 plate with clip

1x5x4 inverted arch

1x2 plate with angled bar handles

This is a minifigure's plume feather

The wings fit onto these plates with clips

FEATHERED FEATURES

This bird is ready to shake its tail feathers! Attach a plate with handles to the back of the roof bricks and clip three pink feathers to it. To complete the bird's head, add a round tile eyeball and a curved slope beak.

OLD BOOT HOUSE

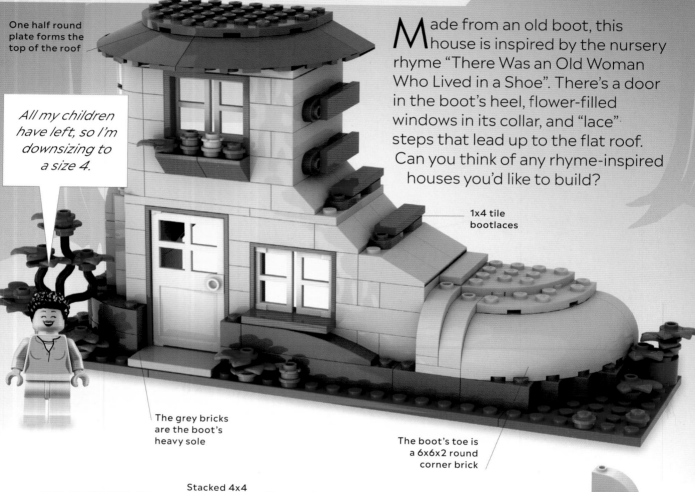

One half round plate forms the top of the roof

All my children have left, so I'm downsizing to a size 4.

Made from an old boot, this house is inspired by the nursery rhyme "There Was an Old Woman Who Lived in a Shoe". There's a door in the boot's heel, flower-filled windows in its collar, and "lace" steps that lead up to the flat roof. Can you think of any rhyme-inspired houses you'd like to build?

1x4 tile bootlaces

The grey bricks are the boot's heavy sole

The boot's toe is a 6x6x2 round corner brick

FOOTPRINT

The grey sole of the old boot is, fittingly, the foundations of the house. The heel gets its rounded shape from 4x4 macaroni bricks, while the shape of the toe is made by offsetting 1x3 bricks. Leave space in the sole for the doorway.

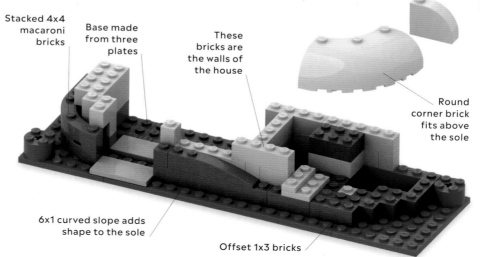

Stacked 4x4 macaroni bricks

Base made from three plates

These bricks are the walls of the house

Round corner brick fits above the sole

6x1 curved slope adds shape to the sole

Offset 1x3 bricks

1x12x3 arch

These stepped slope bricks are the laced-up bit of the boot

BOOT ROOM

The bottom of the boot is the lower room of the house. Add a window and door and a large arch at the back to keep it open for play. Also build up the toe with round plates and slope pieces.

3x1x2 curved slope

2x2 inverted slope

4x6 plate floor

Pieces for the laces will attach here

COLLAR FLOOR

The upstairs room of the boot house is inside the collar. Its red windowsills jut out of the walls thanks to inverted slope bricks.

Stacked macaroni bricks make this curved wall

The bottom two tiles lie flat

LACE IT UP

Once the top floor is complete with windows and flower boxes, the old boot house is ready for some laces! Two 1x2 rounded plates underneath each tile lace look like the holes the laces thread through.

Leave the outside stud exposed

6x6 round corner brick with sloping sides

3x2 slope brick

Add more greenery in the garden as a finishing touch

ROUND ROOF

This boot is built to be lived in, not worn, so it needs a roof at the top of the collar. The round roof has a first layer made from two sloped round corner bricks and two slope bricks.

OUTDOOR FEATURES

F ill your LEGO houses' exteriors with functional and fun details to make the outside spaces just as inviting as the indoor ones. Think of places where your minifigures and their animals can potter, play, dine, and relax.

DOG KENNEL

This small shelter is for a four-legged friend. It even has a paved path that's the perfect size for paws.

Tiled roof made from curved bricks and slopes

1x4 arch brick doorway

6x8 base plate

1x1 half circle tile

Where did I put that hot dog?

This is what happens when you cook near my kennel.

The hood moves on a clip-and-bar connection

1x1 brick with two side studs

Printed 1x1 round tile

Mechanical claw piece is serving tongs

Legs are 1x2 plates with handle bars

BARBEQUE

Your minifigures can sizzle sausages in the garden on this barbeque, then eat them al fresco! Its middle part is made from four 1x1 bricks with two sideways-facing studs. The temperature gauges, legs, and barbeque hood all fit onto their studs.

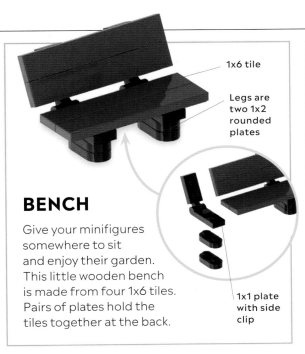

1x6 tile

Legs are two 1x2 rounded plates

BENCH

Give your minifigures somewhere to sit and enjoy their garden. This little wooden bench is made from four 1x6 tiles. Pairs of plates hold the tiles together at the back.

1x1 plate with side clip

LAWNMOWER

There are always lots of jobs to do in a garden, such as cutting the grass. This lawnmower rolls around on two sets of skateboard wheels attached to plates with clips.

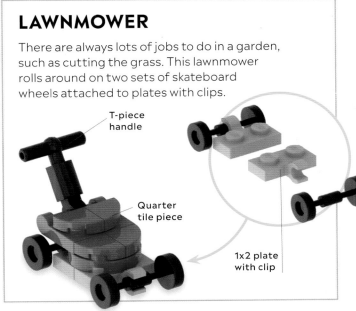

T-piece handle

Quarter tile piece

1x2 plate with clip

FOUNTAIN

A fountain can be the calming centrepiece of a garden. Water made from transparent blue pieces flows down the three layers of this pretty fountain.

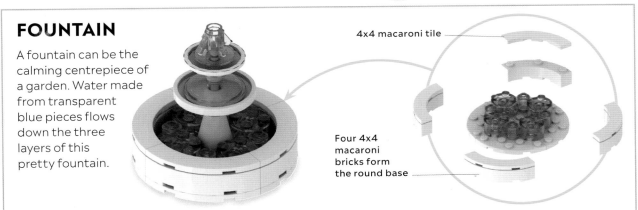

4x4 macaroni tile

Four 4x4 macaroni bricks form the round base

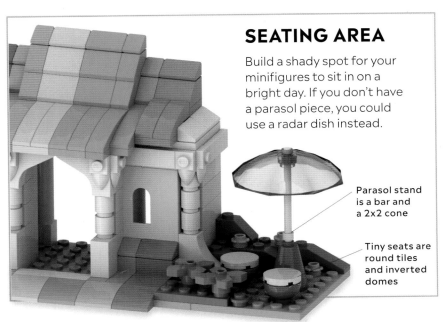

SEATING AREA

Build a shady spot for your minifigures to sit in on a bright day. If you don't have a parasol piece, you could use a radar dish instead.

Parasol stand is a bar and a 2x2 cone

Tiny seats are round tiles and inverted domes

Two 1x2 slopes form the roof

1x2 brick with hole

BIRDHOUSE

Birds need houses, too! An open hole in a 1x2 brick makes the perfect entrance for feathered friends.

2x2 radar dish base

JUNGLE HUT

Tan and dark tan slope bricks form the bamboo roof

Green whips are jungle vines

This little hut can be found deep in the jungle, surrounded by all kinds of plant and animal life. You could easily miss it, as it blends in with its surroundings and even has jungle foliage growing inside and around it. It's raised off the ground on sturdy wooden stilts.

I hope he has porridge.

Bar piece

Wow, I think this may be a new species.

Plants in different sizes make wild jungle foliage

This pillar is a tree trunk

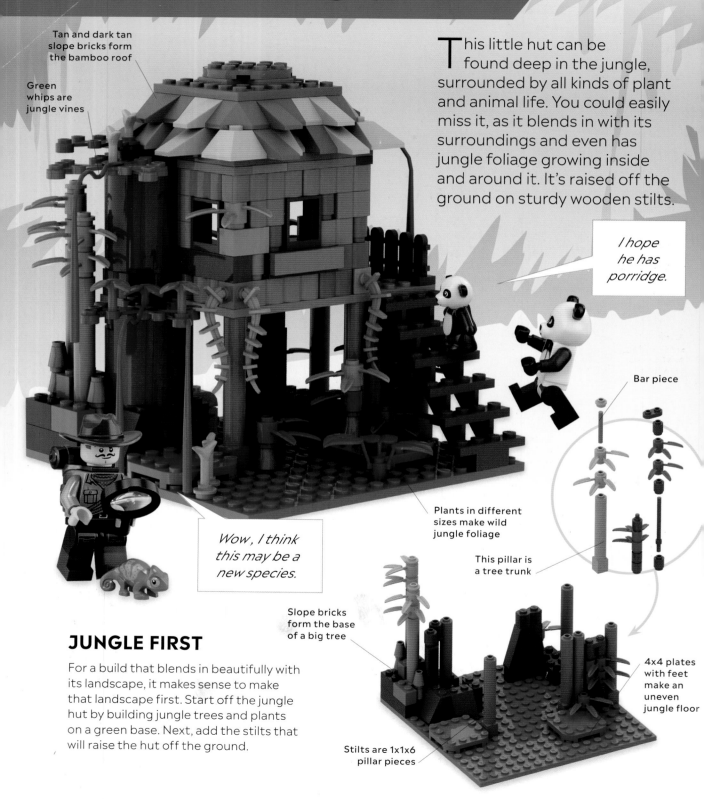

Slope bricks form the base of a big tree

4x4 plates with feet make an uneven jungle floor

JUNGLE FIRST

For a build that blends in beautifully with its landscape, it makes sense to make that landscape first. Start off the jungle hut by building jungle trees and plants on a green base. Next, add the stilts that will raise the hut off the ground.

Stilts are 1x1x6 pillar pieces

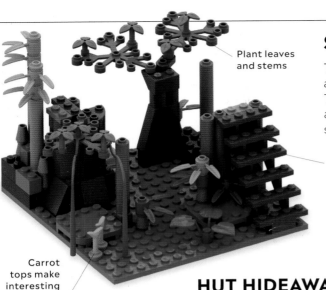

Plant leaves
and stems

STEP IT UP

This jungle is growing rapidly! Now there
are even more trees, plants, and vines.
There may not be a hut yet, but the steps
are there already. They fit onto a sturdy
section of stilts and jungle plants.

Stairs are
all one
piece

This tree trunk
is growing
with the hut

2x2 round
brick log

Balcony
fence

1x2
palisade
brick

Carrot
tops make
interesting
jungle plants

HUT HIDEAWAY

The plate floor of the hut is now in
place and the walls are taking shape.
They're made from a combination of
curvy palisade bricks and round
bricks to create a log effect.

Ceiling plate
is the same
dimensions
as the hut

All kinds of
plant pieces
can be used
for a jungle

1x8 plate is
the top of the
doorframe

These vines hang from
bricks with side studs

CEILING

Once the walls are finished and
topped with plates, it's time
to attach the hut's square 8x8
plate ceiling. While the walls were
growing, the jungle foliage was too!

2x2 wedge
slope

3x1 slope

An extra layer of
plates attaches
here to finish
off the roof

BAMBOO ROOF

Bamboo is a jungle plant with a very hard
stem that is often used to make roofs in
hot countries. The two layers of small slope
pieces in the jungle hut's roof overlap each
other so they look like thatched bamboo.

FANTASY CASTLE

Castles don't need to be big to be spectacular! The pristine white towers and golden spires of this microscale fantasy castle are as awe-inspiring as any regular-sized royal residence. It is perched high on a rocky mountaintop so its minuscule residents can look out for minifigure-scale invaders.

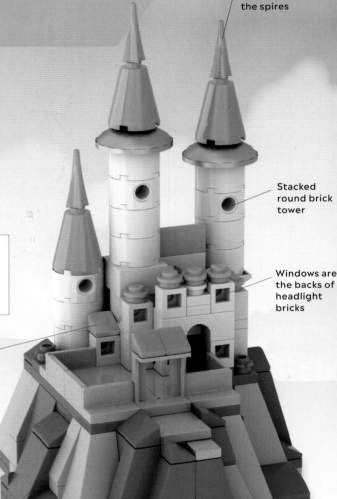

Spear tip pieces form the tops of the spires

Stacked round brick tower

Windows are the backs of headlight bricks

This castle will be mine, even if I can't fit inside!

Tiny 1x1 slope rooftop

Craggy surface formed from slope pieces in various sizes

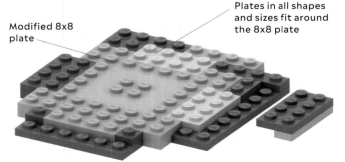

Modified 8x8 plate

Plates in all shapes and sizes fit around the 8x8 plate

ROCKY START

Before building the fantasy castle, make the mountaintop it stands proudly upon. The rocky terrain has a characteristically uneven base, which is built around an 8x8 plate with cutout parts.

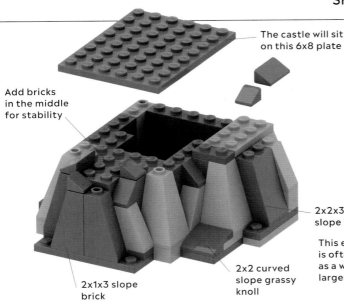

The castle will sit on this 6x8 plate

Add bricks in the middle for stability

2x2x3 slope brick

This entrance is often used as a window on larger castles

2x1x3 slope brick

2x2 curved slope grassy knoll

MAJESTIC MOUNTAIN

Carve the jagged surface of the mountain out of slope bricks in two shades of grey. Add small green pieces among the grey bricks to make small sections of grass and moss on the rocks.

Each square window is the back of a headlight brick

Tile steps built into the mountain

CASTLE WALLS

The castle is now emerging from the rocks. It has solid square walls with a large entrance. Inside the walls, there's a smooth courtyard and the first layer of the castle buildings.

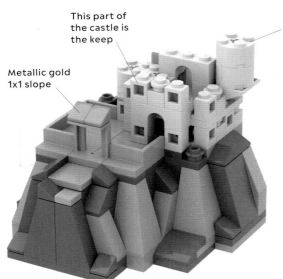

This part of the castle is the keep

Metallic gold 1x1 slope

The start of a 2x2 round brick tower

GRAND DETAILS

The castle keep and other buildings are taking shape. Metallic gold cheese slopes above the entrance and on some of the castle rooftops make this castle look even more grand.

The larger towers have radar dish roofs

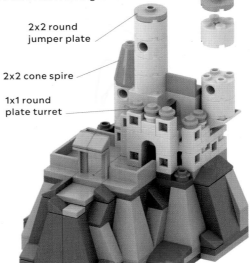

2x2 round jumper plate

2x2 cone spire

1x1 round plate turret

NOT-SO-TALL TOWERS

An entire castle tower can be made from three or four round bricks at microscale. The fantasy castle has three gold-topped towers with windows made from holes in some of the round bricks.

FIXTURES AND FITTINGS

Part of the fun of building a LEGO® house is creating items to play with inside it. Think about how your minifigures will use the interiors of their new home and design the functional spaces, equipment, and little luxuries they might need.

HAMBURGER KITCHEN

Theme your interiors around the style of your house. It's no surprise that the hamburger house's interiors are filled with fast-food-friendly kitchen equipment!

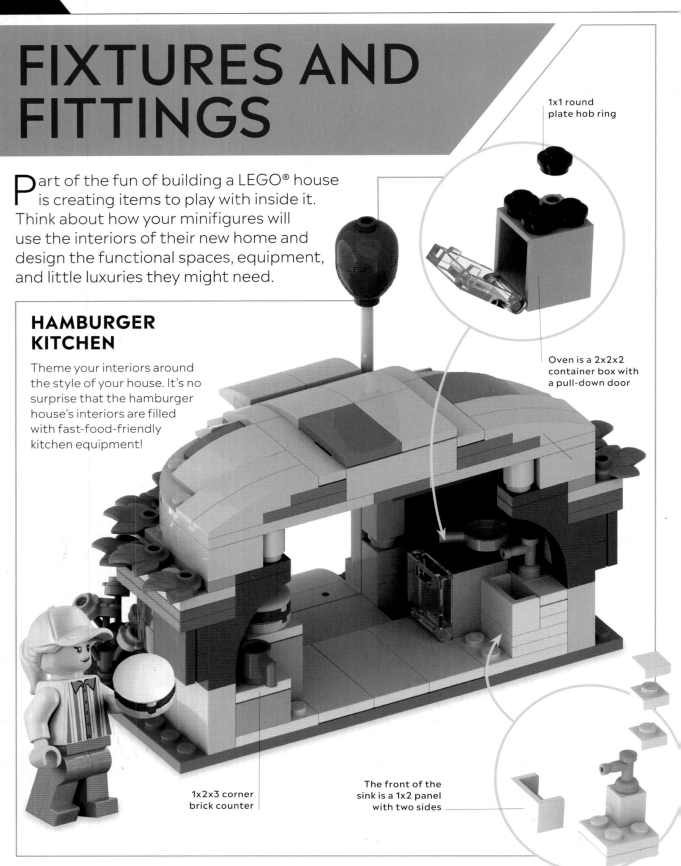

1x1 round plate hob ring

Oven is a 2x2x2 container box with a pull-down door

1x2x3 corner brick counter

The front of the sink is a 1x2 panel with two sides

KITCHEN COUNTER

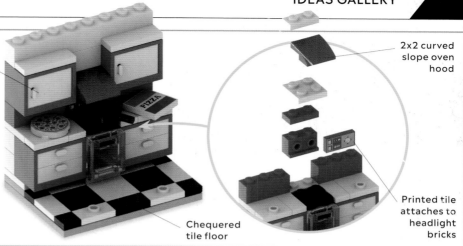

2x3x2 cupboard piece is built into the wall

2x2 curved slope oven hood

Printed tile attaches to headlight bricks

Chequered tile floor

This fitted kitchen has everything in one – cupboards, drawers, and an oven. But it looks like its minifigure owners prefer a takeaway pizza to cooking!

KITCHEN SINK

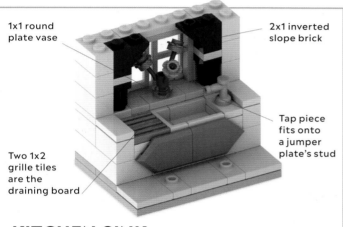

1x1 round plate vase

2x1 inverted slope brick

Two 1x2 grille tiles are the draining board

Tap piece fits onto a jumper plate's stud

This looks like a nice place to wash up! As well as a wide sink, this kitchen fixture has a draining board for drying dishes and bright flowers on the windowsill.

SHOWER

Rub-a-dub-dub! Build your minifigures a shower to make them feel factory fresh. This one has a powerful-looking showerhead made from a radar dish.

1x1 rounded plate with handle

Rainbow-printed tiles

1x2x6 brick shower screen

TOILET

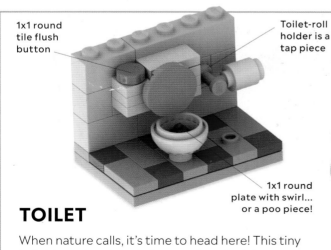

1x1 round tile flush button

Toilet-roll holder is a tap piece

1x1 round plate with swirl... or a poo piece!

When nature calls, it's time to head here! This tiny toilet has a bowl made from an inverted dome, a round tile lid, and a well-placed round brick toilet roll.

Did I forget to flush?

MEDIEVAL INN

Black pieces for the stained wood frame

Inns or taverns like this one were places where the minifigures of medieval Europe would gather to rest and feast. This inn is a traditional half-timbered building, which means it has a wooden frame that's filled with brick or stone. It has an overhanging upper storey to hurl rubbish or insults from!

I've heard better...

Outdoor store for casks of ale

A round and a square tile form the well-worn doorstep

Wooden window surrounds made from cones, round bricks, and plates

The bottom of the building is made from bricks

To build... or not to build...

This wall will only be seen from the inside

Low wall for the outdoor store

A window will fit above here

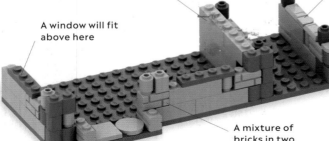

A mixture of bricks in two shades of grey looks like natural stone

The doorstep is built on a 1x6 plate

STONE BASE

While the top half of the medieval inn has a wooden frame, the bottom half is made from stone. The whole building covers its base plate, with no extra space around the edges, because this medieval building would be right next to other houses on a street.

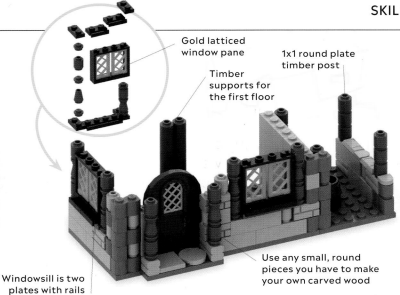

Gold latticed window pane

1x1 round plate timber post

Timber supports for the first floor

Windowsill is two plates with rails

Use any small, round pieces you have to make your own carved wood

TIMBER DETAILS

Now the windows and door are fixed inside the walls along with more timber details. There are carved wood panels on either side of the windows and a matching frame around the door.

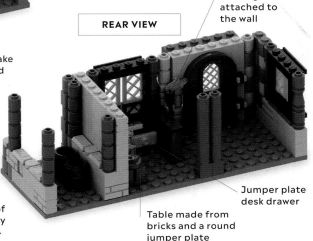

REAR VIEW

Flaming torch attached to the wall

Jumper plate desk drawer

Table made from bricks and a round jumper plate

INSIDE THE INN

Once you have an inn with solid walls, you could add some interior details, such as a desk, cupboards, benches, tables, and lighting, to make it look inviting.

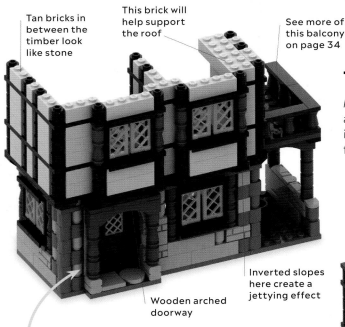

Tan bricks in between the timber look like stone

This brick will help support the roof

See more of this balcony on page 34

Wooden arched doorway

Inverted slopes here create a jettying effect

TIMBERED TOP FLOOR

Many medieval buildings have upper floors that are bigger than the floor below, like the inn. This is called "jettying". The inn's timber-framed top floor also has a balcony overlooking the street.

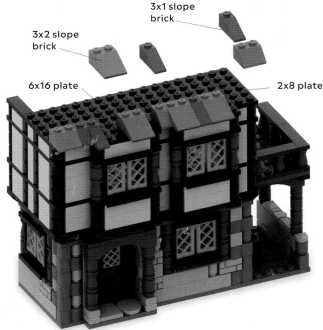

3x1 slope brick

3x2 slope brick

6x16 plate

2x8 plate

TILED ROOF

Complete the medieval inn with a clay tile roof. The slope-brick tiles above the windows are angled slightly differently from the rest to protect the windows from rain and snow.

1x1 cone

LIGHTING

It's time to shine a light on lighting! Without it, your minifigures would have a hard time getting around their homes and streets in the nighttime. Here are some ideas for indoor and outdoor builds that might give you a light-bulb moment.

This is called a "treetop" piece

Candle piece with a tiny flame on top

1x2 rounded plate has two open holes

CANDELABRA

This fancy light is called a candelabra. It's a candle holder with four arms made from rounded plates. A four-pronged connector holds them all together.

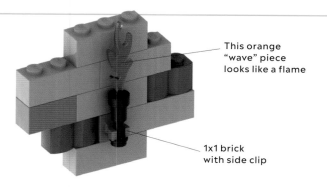

This orange "wave" piece looks like a flame

1x1 brick with side clip

WALL TORCH

Ancient castles or caves are often lit by wall torches that can be removed. This torch is made from a telescope piece, which attaches to a brick with clip built into the wall.

The curves are paint roller pieces!

Hanging lightbulb is a minifigure head

Is it bright in here?

The ornate post is all one piece

LAMPPOST

Without lampposts, how would minifigures find their way home in the dark? This one has a curvy, hanging lamp design.

Radar-dish lampshade

1x1 round plate is the bulb's screw base

FLOOR LAMP

This modern lamp stands on a bar with stopper. The "bulb" that fits on top is a transparent minifigure head!

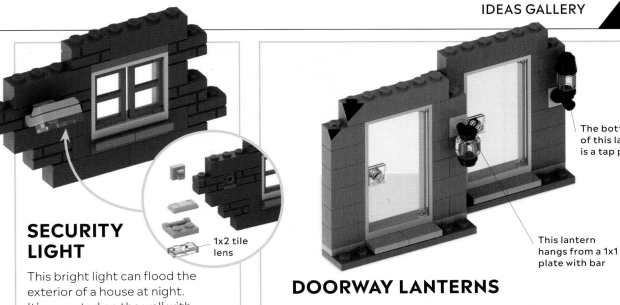

SECURITY LIGHT

This bright light can flood the exterior of a house at night. It's mounted on the wall with a headlight brick's side stud.

1x2 tile lens

DOORWAY LANTERNS

Add lanterns to the outside of your house's doorways, so your minifigures can always find their keys in the dark. These three lantern designs fit onto side studs in the wall.

The bottom of this lamp is a tap piece

This lantern hangs from a 1x1 plate with bar

Radar dish shade directs light to the path

GARDEN LIGHTS

These little low lights can illuminate a garden path. Stylishly simple, they're each made from just three pieces.

Slurp!

1x1 brick with side stud

TREEHOUSE

U p on the top perch of this treehouse, high among the canopy of the surrounding trees, your minifigures can escape the modern world and get back to nature. Perhaps too much so! It has two platforms that are built out of the thick tree trunk and a rope for climbing up and down.

I'd better go now, Chimpy.

Round corner brick roof

Kevin, your boss is on the phone. She's wondering why you aren't at work.

Minifigures can hold onto this hanging rope

Branches are plant leaf pieces

Slope brick tree root

Stacked 2x2 round bricks

2x1x2 slope brick

Layered round plates make an uneven forest floor

PUTTING DOWN ROOTS

Build gnarly tree roots from any slope bricks and rounded bricks you have in your collection. The bricks in the middle of the trunk won't be seen on the final model so they can be any colour you like.

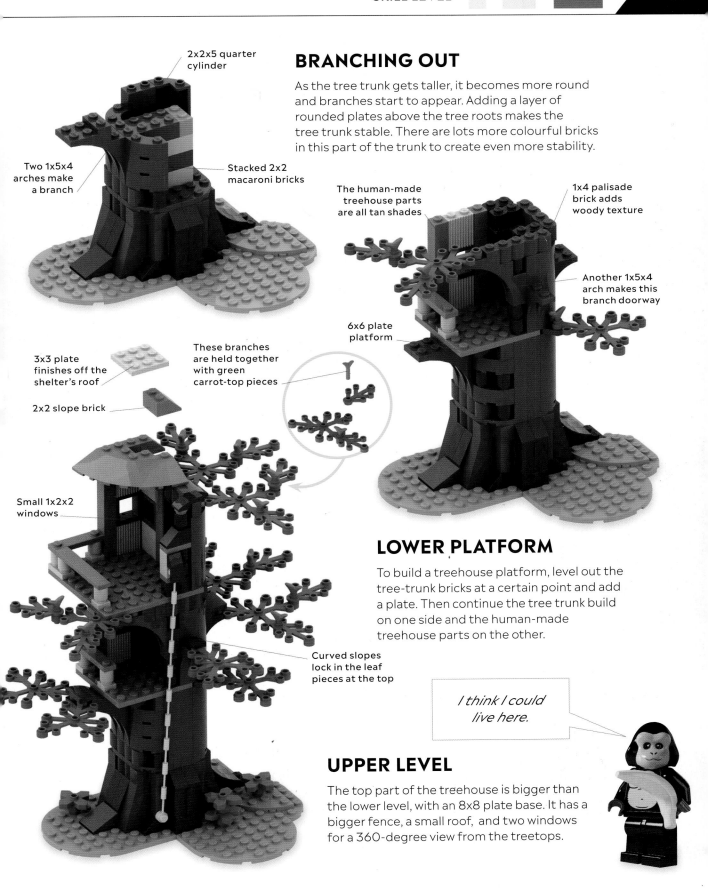

2x2x5 quarter cylinder

BRANCHING OUT

As the tree trunk gets taller, it becomes more round and branches start to appear. Adding a layer of rounded plates above the tree roots makes the tree trunk stable. There are lots more colourful bricks in this part of the trunk to create even more stability.

Two 1x5x4 arches make a branch

Stacked 2x2 macaroni bricks

The human-made treehouse parts are all tan shades

1x4 palisade brick adds woody texture

Another 1x5x4 arch makes this branch doorway

6x6 plate platform

3x3 plate finishes off the shelter's roof

These branches are held together with green carrot-top pieces

2x2 slope brick

LOWER PLATFORM

To build a treehouse platform, level out the tree-trunk bricks at a certain point and add a plate. Then continue the tree trunk build on one side and the human-made treehouse parts on the other.

Small 1x2x2 windows

Curved slopes lock in the leaf pieces at the top

I think I could live here.

UPPER LEVEL

The top part of the treehouse is bigger than the lower level, with an 8x8 plate base. It has a bigger fence, a small roof, and two windows for a 360-degree view from the treetops.

MEDIEVAL CASTLE

Real-life medieval castles were built to stand in place for centuries, but a LEGO castle can be changed around regularly to suit its royal residents' needs! This imposing castle has two turrets, red and gold banners, and a catapult to scare away anyone who wants to capture it.

The winner will marry my pet frog!

Erm, I'm not sure about this...

Modified 3x3 bricks shape the castle turrets

Banners hang from a bar piece attached to clips

Olive pieces give the walls an aged look

See pages 22-23 for more castle window ideas

Palisade bricks add a stony texture to the walls

CASTLE PLOT

Begin the castle by plotting out where the gate, turrets, and walls will go on a base plate. At this point, you could also add in smaller details like a well-worn path and flaming torches inside.

1x1x6 pillar

Flaming torches clipped to the inside walls

8x16 base plate

Different-sized tiles look like worn-down stones

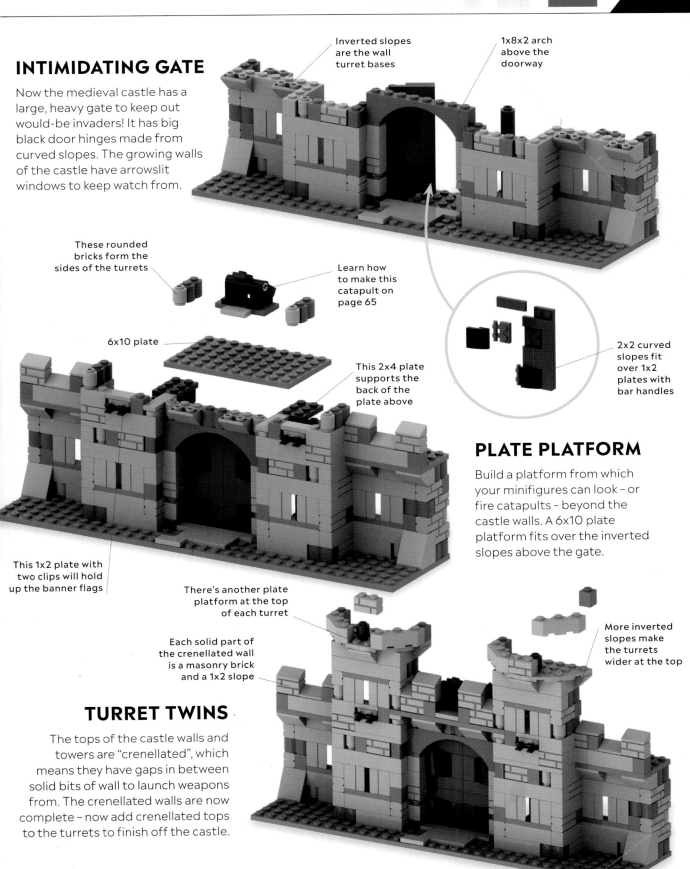

INTIMIDATING GATE

Now the medieval castle has a large, heavy gate to keep out would-be invaders! It has big black door hinges made from curved slopes. The growing walls of the castle have arrowslit windows to keep watch from.

Inverted slopes are the wall turret bases

1x8x2 arch above the doorway

These rounded bricks form the sides of the turrets

Learn how to make this catapult on page 65

2x2 curved slopes fit over 1x2 plates with bar handles

6x10 plate

This 2x4 plate supports the back of the plate above

PLATE PLATFORM

Build a platform from which your minifigures can look – or fire catapults – beyond the castle walls. A 6x10 plate platform fits over the inverted slopes above the gate.

This 1x2 plate with two clips will hold up the banner flags

There's another plate platform at the top of each turret

Each solid part of the crenellated wall is a masonry brick and a 1x2 slope

More inverted slopes make the turrets wider at the top

TURRET TWINS

The tops of the castle walls and towers are "crenellated", which means they have gaps in between solid bits of wall to launch weapons from. The crenellated walls are now complete – now add crenellated tops to the turrets to finish off the castle.

FURNITURE

Even minifigures like to flop down on a soft-looking sofa after a hard day's work! Adding moveable items like chairs, tables, beds, and cupboards will bring comfort and character to the interiors of your LEGO homes.

Don't forget to make your bed!

BED

1x4x1 bow window

4x6 plate bed base

1x1 cheese slopes form the edges of the duvet

1x1 plate bedknob

Give your minifigures a warm bed to come home to. This single one has a smooth tile and cheese slope duvet, and a headboard made from a bow window piece.

SIDEBOARD

A sideboard is often the place where the best glasses, plates, and cutlery in the house are stored. This sideboard is particularly grand-looking, with carved wood and gold drawers and details.

Two headlight bricks hold each drawer in place

4x1 curved slopes make it rounded at the top

1x1 plate with swirl

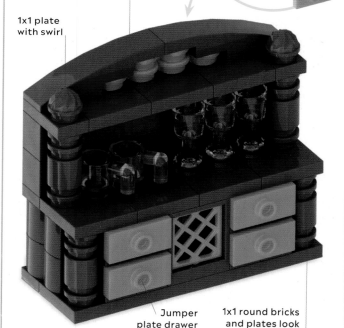

Jumper plate drawer

1x1 round bricks and plates look like carved wood

SOFA

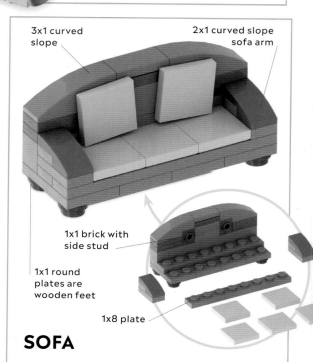

3x1 curved slope

2x1 curved slope sofa arm

1x1 brick with side stud

1x1 round plates are wooden feet

1x8 plate

This brightly coloured LEGO sofa may not be soft, but it's perfectly suited to a minifigure's needs. It has tile cushions attached to sideways-facing studs built into the back of the sofa.

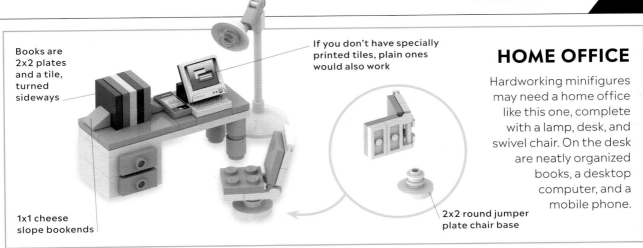

HOME OFFICE

Hardworking minifigures may need a home office like this one, complete with a lamp, desk, and swivel chair. On the desk are neatly organized books, a desktop computer, and a mobile phone.

Books are 2x2 plates and a tile, turned sideways

If you don't have specially printed tiles, plain ones would also work

1x1 cheese slope bookends

2x2 round jumper plate chair base

COFFEE TABLE

This tiny table has two jumper plates on the top to attach a mug of coffee and a plate of biscuits to!

It looks like someone has taken one already!

1x2 rounded plate table legs

2x4 plate

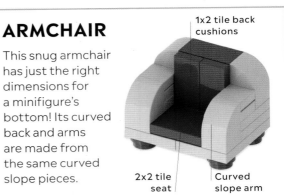

ARMCHAIR

This snug armchair has just the right dimensions for a minifigure's bottom! Its curved back and arms are made from the same curved slope pieces.

1x2 tile back cushions

2x2 tile seat

Curved slope arm

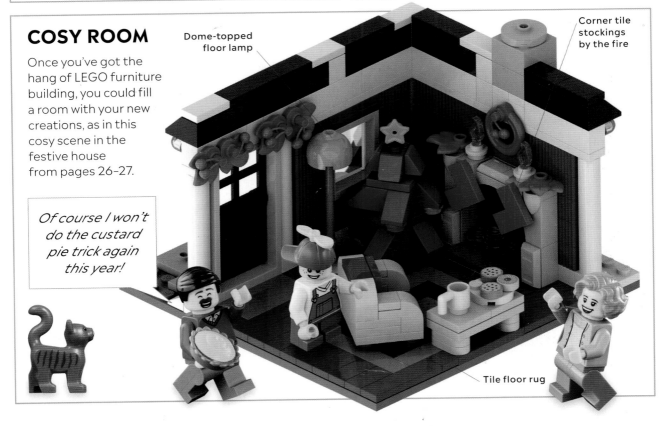

COSY ROOM

Once you've got the hang of LEGO furniture building, you could fill a room with your new creations, as in this cosy scene in the festive house from pages 26–27.

Of course I won't do the custard pie trick again this year!

Dome-topped floor lamp

Corner tile stockings by the fire

Tile floor rug

HAUNTED HOUSE

Take care if you step beyond the tall iron gates of this home – it's the kind of place where things go bump in the night. With a creepy colour scheme, a shadowy basement, and a creaky old tree in the garden, this haunted house is sure to be filled with hidden horrors.

No cheese, please – it gives me nightmares.

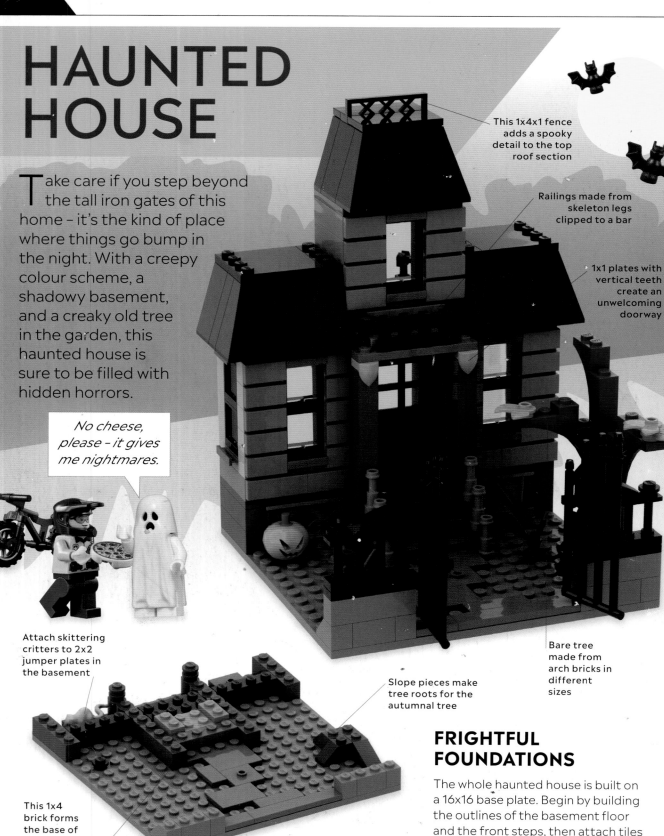

This 1x4x1 fence adds a spooky detail to the top roof section

Railings made from skeleton legs clipped to a bar

1x1 plates with vertical teeth create an unwelcoming doorway

Bare tree made from arch bricks in different sizes

Attach skittering critters to 2x2 jumper plates in the basement

Slope pieces make tree roots for the autumnal tree

This 1x4 brick forms the base of the second step

FRIGHTFUL FOUNDATIONS

The whole haunted house is built on a 16x16 base plate. Begin by building the outlines of the basement floor and the front steps, then attach tiles to the front of the base plate to create a jaggedly winding garden path.

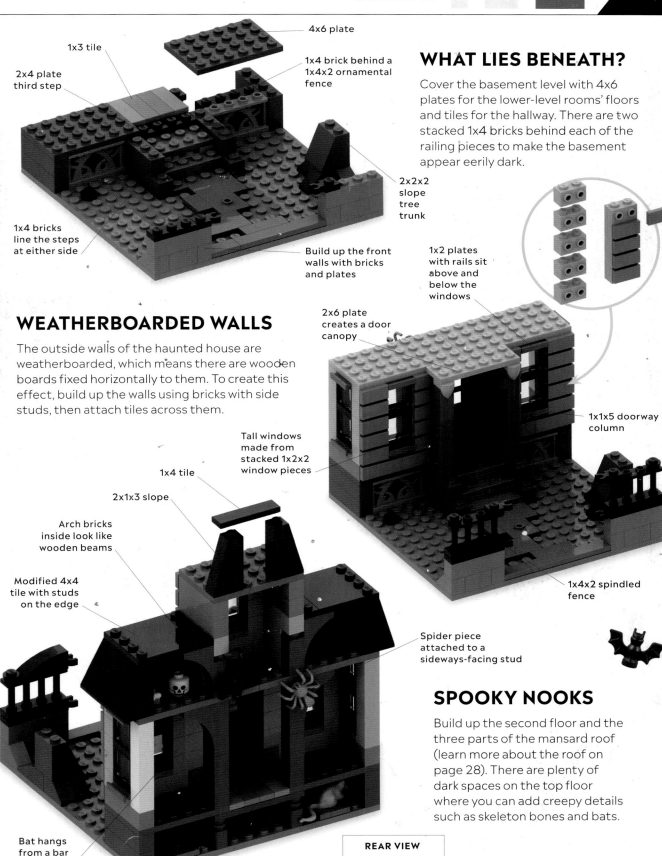

4x6 plate

1x3 tile

2x4 plate
third step

1x4 brick behind a
1x4x2 ornamental
fence

1x4 bricks
line the steps
at either side

2x2x2
slope
tree
trunk

Build up the front
walls with bricks
and plates

WHAT LIES BENEATH?

Cover the basement level with 4x6
plates for the lower-level rooms' floors
and tiles for the hallway. There are two
stacked 1x4 bricks behind each of the
railing pieces to make the basement
appear eerily dark.

1x2 plates
with rails sit
above and
below the
windows

2x6 plate
creates a door
canopy

1x1x5 doorway
column

WEATHERBOARDED WALLS

The outside walls of the haunted house are
weatherboarded, which means there are wooden
boards fixed horizontally to them. To create this
effect, build up the walls using bricks with side
studs, then attach tiles across them.

Tall windows
made from
stacked 1x2x2
window pieces

1x4 tile

2x1x3 slope

Arch bricks
inside look like
wooden beams

Modified 4x4
tile with studs
on the edge

1x4x2 spindled
fence

Spider piece
attached to a
sideways-facing stud

SPOOKY NOOKS

Build up the second floor and the
three parts of the mansard roof
(learn more about the roof on
page 28). There are plenty of
dark spaces on the top floor
where you can add creepy details
such as skeleton bones and bats.

Bat hangs
from a bar
in the wall

REAR VIEW

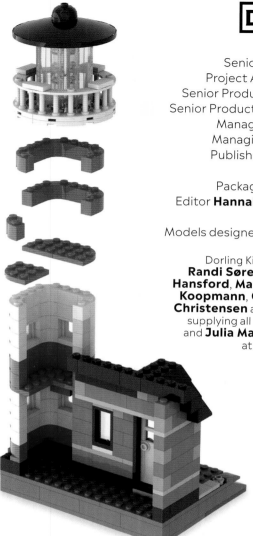

DK | Penguin Random House

Senior Editor **Helen Murray**
Project Art Editor **Jenny Edwards**
Senior Production Editor **Jennifer Murray**
Senior Production Controller **Louise Minihane**
Managing Editor **Paula Regan**
Managing Art Editor **Jo Connor**
Publishing Director **Mark Searle**

Packaged for DK by **Plum Jam**
Editor **Hannah Dolan**   Designer **Guy Harvey**

Models designed and created by **Jessica Farrell**

Dorling Kindersley would like to thank:
**Randi Sørensen, Heidi K. Jensen, Paul
Hansford, Martin Leighton Lindhardt, Nina
Koopmann, Charlotte Neidhardt,** and **Lis
Christensen** at the LEGO Group; **Nate Dias** for
supplying all model images and breakdowns;
and **Julia March** and **Jennette ElNaggar**
at DK for proofreading.

Manufactured by Dorling Kindersley, One Embassy
Gardens, 8 Viaduct Gardens, London SW11 7BW,
under licence from the LEGO Group.

10 9 8 7 6 5 4 3 2 1
001-324043-Oct/2021

First published in Great Britain in 2021 by
Dorling Kindersley Limited
DK, One Embassy Gardens, 8 Viaduct Gardens,
London SW11 7BW

The authorised representative in the EEA is
Dorling Kindersley Verlag GmbH. Arnulfstr. 124,
80636 Munich, Germany

Page design copyright ©2021
Dorling Kindersley Limited
A Penguin Random House Company

A CIP catalogue record for this book
is available from the British Library.
ISBN: 978-0-2415-0627-1

Printed and bound in China

For the curious
www.dk.com/legohouses

www.LEGO.com

MIX
Paper from
responsible sources
FSC™ C018179

This book was made with
Forest Stewardship Council™
certified paper – one small
step in DK's commitment to
a sustainable future.